Springtime of the Spirit

Homilies for the Weekdays of Lent and Holy Week

Cover: *The Sacred Tree*, a sculpture in weathered, distressed steel; gold leaf; and handmade paper. By David Orth. www.orthsculpture.com. Image used with permission.

Scripture quotations are from the New Revised Standard Version of the Bible, copyright © 1989 the National Council of the Churches of Christ in the USA. Used by permission. All rights reserved. Psalm passages are from the Psalter in *The Book of Common Prayer*.

© 2016 Forward Movement

ISBN: 9780880284349

Printed in USA

Forward
Movement

Springtime
of the Spirit

Homilies for the Weekdays
of Lent and Holy Week

John D. Alexander

Forward Movement
Cincinnati, Ohio

Introduction

The Christian calendar divides the church year into liturgical seasons, punctuated by joyful feasts and solemn fasts. As finite creatures with limited attention spans, we cannot absorb the multifaceted splendor of the whole faith at once, so the church calendar focuses our gaze now on this aspect or theme, now on that. As we repeat the cycle year after year, our appreciation of the total picture grows, and we gradually become a people who have lives and identities cumulatively shaped by the successive mysteries that the church calendar sets before us.

The preeminent celebration of the church year, the Feast of the Resurrection at Easter, is preceded by the preparatory and penitential season of Lent, which extends properly from Ash Wednesday through Maundy Thursday. The Easter Triduum—beginning with the Maundy Thursday liturgy, moving into Good Friday, and on through the Great Vigil—is the most profound and sacred time of the church year. The word Lent comes from an old English word for spring, possibly connected to the "lengthening" of days. Traditionally reckoned as forty days, the season originated as a time of preparation for baptism at Easter and, by extension, of spiritual renewal for all Christians. Many parishes and church communities break the Lenten fast at the Eucharistic celebration observed during the Great Vigil of Easter, after sundown on Holy Saturday.

One time-honored Lenten practice is increased participation in the Church's offerings of liturgical worship, including recitation of the Offices and attendance at weekday celebrations of the Holy Eucharist. The homilies in this book accompany The Episcopal Church's Eucharistic Lectionary for "The Weekdays of Lent," which appears in *Lesser Feasts and Fasts* (2006), and gives a Collect, Old Testament Reading, Psalm, and Gospel for each weekday of the season. This Episcopal lectionary comes from the 1985 Lectionary of the Anglican Church of Canada, which was adapted in turn from the 1970 *Roman Missal*.

Also included in this volume are homilies for Ash Wednesday and the daily liturgies of Holy Week through the Great Vigil of Easter, as appointed in *The Book of Common Prayer, 1979*. I have not included the Liturgy of the Word for Holy Saturday or attempted to provide sermons for the Sundays of Lent or Palm Sunday, which follow the three-year cycle of the Revised Common Lectionary.

My hope is that this book will be useful to preachers in cathedrals, churches, and chapels who may find themselves presiding at weekday celebrations of the Holy Eucharist during the Lenten Season. Such preachers likely will want to use these homilies as a starting point for their own reflections and applications to the life of their congregations. I am offering what I hope will be a helpful first word (but certainly not the last word) on the daily biblical texts.

This book may also be used for individual or group reflection. In this case, the readings and psalm (and, if possible, the Collect) for the day should be read slowly and meditatively—possibly aloud to the group or to oneself—prior to engaging with the homily. These homilies generally presuppose that the appointed lessons and psalm have just been read, either publicly or privately.

Another use for this book may be as a course of daily Lenten readings for those preparing to receive the sacrament of Baptism at Easter. Again, to get the most out of each homily, the readings and psalm for the day should be read first. These homilies can be used to supplement and enrich this period of study but should certainly not replace a traditional program of pre-baptismal catechesis.

The notes "Concerning the Proper" in *Lesser Feasts and Fasts* contain the following direction on the observation of saints' days during Lent:

> *In keeping with ancient tradition, the observance of*
> *Lenten weekdays ordinarily takes precedence over*
> *Lesser Feasts occurring during this season. It is*

3

appropriate, however, to name the saint whose day it is in the Prayers of the People, and, if desired, to use the Collect of the saint to conclude the Prayers (p. 27).

On such days, the saint's Collect may alternatively be used as the Collect of the Day during Morning Prayer or Evening Prayer.

In the third, fourth, and fifth weeks of Lent, the lectionary offers an Alternative Proper, which may be used on any day of the week, rather than the readings appointed for that day. These three Alternative Propers repeat the gospel readings for the preceding Sundays in Year A of the three-year cycle, and so are especially appropriate for use in Years B and C. They feature specific readings from John's Gospel traditionally used in pre-baptismal catechesis: the Samaritan woman (Third Sunday), the healing of the man born blind (Fourth Sunday), and the raising of Lazarus (Fifth Sunday).

Many of these homilies are based on earlier sermons and homilies that I have given at daily Mass at Saint Stephen's Church in Providence, Rhode Island, over the past sixteen years. This book is dedicated to my parishioners there, in gratitude for their constant encouragement and support.

Ash Wednesday

Joel 2:1-2, 12-17 *or* Isaiah 58:1-12
Psalm 103 *or* 103:8-14
2 Corinthians 5:20b—6:10
Matthew 6:1-6, 16-21

Several decades ago, a phenomenon known as "renewal" arose in the life of the Church. Some of the renewal movements are still around, but their heyday was mostly in the 1970s and 80s.

The basic appeal of these movements was to churchgoers whose faith and practice had grown stale over the years. Often, lifelong parishioners began to realize that their prayer lives had become dry and arid, and their participation in the life of the Church seemed like they were going through the motions, with no deep sense of meaning, reward, fulfillment, or connection. The greatest temptation for many at this point is to simply give up and decide that the Christian faith doesn't mean anything much in one's life anymore. Renewal movements stepped in and said, *No, the solution is not to give up but to renew your faith through a deeper encounter with God in worship and prayer, in study and service.*

The renewal movements typically organized church weekends, retreats, and conferences making use of revivalist techniques such as passionate preaching, personal testimonies offered up by program veterans, small group sharing, and enthusiastic singing with acoustic instruments. At their worst, these movements could be emotionally manipulative, pietistic, and divisive. At their best, they helped bring many people and congregations into more mature, joyful, and robust expressions and experiences of faith.

The problem with these approaches became apparent by the early twenty-first century—sooner or later the exhilaration and enthusiasm of a renewal weekend wears off, and people begin to look for something *more*. The same techniques that initially provided a warm and zealous glow now leave folks cold. At this point, once again, the temptation is to give up. But rather than giving up, many people find themselves turning to classical disciplines and practices of traditional Anglican, Catholic, and Orthodox spirituality: the Daily Office, meditation, fasting, *lectio divina*, confession, the Rosary, Eucharistic adoration, retreats, pilgrimages, and spiritual direction. Such time-tested practices undergird the real foundation for a vital and vibrant Christian faith.

Lent may profitably be thought of as the Church's annual season of spiritual renewal. Every year, we are invited to renew—more precisely, we are invited to let the Holy Spirit renew—our Christian faith and practice by means of the traditional disciplines of prayer, fasting, and almsgiving.

In today's Gospel, Jesus warns us against making a public show of our Lenten disciplines: "Beware of practicing your piety before others in order to be seen by them; for then you have no reward from your Father in heaven." His words assume, however, that his hearers *will* be undertaking these disciplines. He does not say "if" but "when" you fast, pray, and give alms—this is how to go about it. Fasting, prayer, and almsgiving are not optional in the Christian life.

If we've not already done so, then it behooves us to commit ourselves to a simple rule comprising these three elements for the Lenten season:

Prayer and worship: We take on some additional form of prayer every day in addition to faithful attendance at worship on Sundays.

Fasting and abstinence: Contrary to what we may have been told during the past thirty years or so, Lent involves not just "taking something on," but also "giving something up." Self-denial is an essential component of any Lenten rule.

Almsgiving: Ideally in connection with whatever we give up, we take on some form of financial or material generosity to those less fortunate than ourselves.

A good Lenten rule will combine and hold in tension two characteristics. First, it should be challenging enough that keeping the rule requires some effort—indeed personal sacrifice—to fulfill. But second, the rule should be simple and achievable. Better to commit to an easier rule and keep it, than to commit to a more difficult rule and fail.

The ashes we receive today signify our commitment to repent and return to the Lord. The Lenten disciplines of prayer, fasting, and almsgiving lay the foundations of true spiritual renewal. If we keep them faithfully, we will find our faith growing and deepening. And the joy of Easter will be so much greater in the end.

Thursday after Ash Wednesday

Deuteronomy 30:15-20
Psalm 1
Luke 9:18-25

Lent is often likened to a journey or pilgrimage. In this illustration, we can imagine Thursday, Friday, and Saturday following Ash Wednesday as the time of initial preparations. Yesterday, on Ash Wednesday we committed ourselves to the journey. Between now and Sunday, we find ourselves still in the staging area, gathering together before setting out on the long journey.

Yesterday, we sought to make a good beginning of Lent. Today, we pause to consider the two roads before us.

Today's Old Testament reading from Deuteronomy presents this choice in stark terms. Moses addresses the Hebrews at the end of their forty years of wandering in the wilderness, as they are about to cross the Jordan into the Promised Land. "See, I have set before you today life and prosperity, death and adversity" (30:15). If the people walk in the ways of the Lord, and obey his laws, then they will prosper and multiply, and the Lord will bless them in the land they are entering. But if their hearts turn away, and they worship and serve other gods, they shall perish and not live long in the land the Lord has given over for their possession.

Psalm 1 echoes a similar theme, contrasting the "way of the righteous" with the "way of the wicked." The righteous are like "trees planted by streams of water, bearing fruit in due season, with leaves that do not wither; everything they do shall prosper" (1:3). The wicked, by contrast, are like "chaff which the wind blows away;" they "shall not stand upright when judgment comes" (1:4, 5).

Our readings from Deuteronomy and Psalms present simple equations of cause and effect: Virtue leads to prosperity and blessing; vice leads to punishment and ruin. However, by New Testament times, this equation no longer seemed credible. The world was full of wicked people who enjoyed huge material prosperity and blessings. Many righteous people suffered cruelly at the hands of wicked rulers and oppressive regimes. "Why do the wicked prosper and the righteous suffer?" had become an urgent philosophical and theological question for the contemporaries of Jesus and the disciples.

In today's Gospel, Jesus makes clear that his way is not one that will bring health, wealth, or earthly blessings—at least not in this world. Even though Jesus is "the Christ of God," nonetheless he must "undergo great suffering, and be rejected by the elders, chief priests, and scribes, and be killed, and on the third day be raised." Similarly, his disciples are called to follow in the way of the cross: "If any want to become my followers, let them deny themselves, and take up their cross daily and follow me."

The choice Jesus sets before us is between the world and life. Those who try to save their lives will lose them, and those who lose their lives for Jesus' sake will save them. (The Greek word for life is *psyche*, which can equally well be translated as soul or self.) The Christian life entails taking up our crosses and following Jesus in the trust that even when we seem to be losing everything in this world, we are in fact saving our lives, our selves, and our very souls.

Every year, Lent affords us the opportunity to practice walking the way of the cross by means of the spiritual disciplines we take on, so that when our Lord asks us to make sacrifices for his sake, we will be physically ready and spiritually prepared. Such is the nature of the Lenten journey we have begun.

Friday after Ash Wednesday

Isaiah 58:1-9a
Psalm 51:1-10
Matthew 9:10-17

We rightly associate Lent with fasting. *The Book of Common Prayer, 1979* identifies Ash Wednesday and Good Friday, which bookend this season, as the two principal fasts of the Church calendar, and the weekdays of Lent as days to be set aside for some form of fasting, abstinence, or self-denial.

We need to understand the nature and purpose of fasting to avoid certain snares and pitfalls. In the Gospel for Ash Wednesday, Jesus has warned us not to make a display of our fasting by looking dismal. When we pray, fast, and give alms to impress others, we have received our reward and have come no closer to God. That is, our prayer, fasting, and almsgiving may succeed in making us look holy and pious in the eyes of others, but achieving that purpose does nothing to strengthen our relationship with God. By contrast, prayer, fasting, and almsgiving done in secret is spiritually profitable for us because God alone is witness (Matthew 6:1-18).

Today's reading from Isaiah elaborates on the distinction between fasting that is pleasing to God and fasting that is not pleasing to God. The people begin by asking why their fasts seem of no consequence to God. Speaking on God's behalf, Isaiah answers back that the people's fasting is superficial—a substitute for signs of true repentance, faith, and obedience: "you serve your own interest on your fast day, and oppress all your workers…you fast only to quarrel and to fight and to strike with a wicked fist" (3-4).

In contrast to such hypocritical kowtowing and malingering in sackcloth and ashes, the Lord desires another kind of fast:

> Is not this the fast that I choose:
> > to loose the bonds of injustice,
> > to undo the thongs of the yoke,
> to let the oppressed go free,
> > and to break every yoke?
> Is it not to share your bread with the hungry,
> > and bring the homeless poor into your house;
> when you see the naked, to cover them,
> > and not to hide yourself from your own kin?
> > (Isaiah 58:6-7)

These lines do not condemn fasting *per se*. But they do make very clear that fasting is ineffectual in bringing us into right relationship with God unless it is accompanied by and becomes a sign of genuine repentance manifested in acts of social justice—caring and advocating for the poor, oppressed, hungry, outcast, naked, and homeless. This type of fasting brings great blessings: "Then you shall call, and the LORD will answer; you shall cry for help, and he will say, Here I am" (Isaiah 58:9). Isaiah's words indicate that our fasting is pleasing to God when it motivates us to help those for whom God specially cares.

In today's Gospel, Jesus explicitly links fasting with mourning. Disciples of John the Baptist ask Jesus, "Why do we and the Pharisees fast often, but your disciples do not fast?" Jesus responds: "The wedding guests cannot mourn as long as the Bridegroom is with them, can they? The days will come when the Bridegroom is taken away from them, and then they will fast" (Matthew 9:14-15).

One implication is that the feasts of the liturgical calendar are the times when we celebrate the nearness or presence of the Bridegroom, the risen Jesus, in and with his Church: above all Easter, but also All Saints, Christmas, Epiphany, Ascension, and Pentecost.

The fasts of the liturgical calendar, by contrast, are the times when we mourn the Lord's distance or absence from his Church. But is the omnipresent Lord really ever absent from the members of his Body on earth? The best answer is no, he is always near us and with us. But we have the capability of removing ourselves from his presence—if only from our awareness of his presence—by our sins.

The Lenten hymn, "Lord, who throughout these forty days," asks the Lord to "teach us with thee to mourn our sins, and close by thee to stay" (#142). We fast during Lent as an expression of mourning—not that the Bridegroom has been removed from us but that by our sins we have removed ourselves from the Bridegroom.

Saturday after Ash Wednesday

Isaiah 58:9b-14
Psalm 86:1-11
Luke 5:27-32

At the heart of Lent is the call to repentance. To observe a holy Lent, our deepest needs are to acknowledge our sinfulness, ask God's forgiveness, and amend our lives.

Today's reading from Isaiah voices God's promise to hear and respond favorably to two specific forms of repentance. First is repentance from social injustice. The children of Israel are called to "remove the yoke...the pointing of the finger...the speaking of evil" (58:9). These phrases most likely refer to the perversion of justice in the courts of law by which the rights of the poor and oppressed are denied by the rich and powerful. Complementing the elimination of injustice is the practice of mercy: The people are called to offer "food to the hungry and satisfy the needs of the afflicted" (58:10).

The second form of repentance is proper observance of the Sabbath. God calls the people to "refrain from trampling the Sabbath, from pursuing your own interests on my holy day" (58:13). Such Sabbath observance furthers the drive toward social justice because it is the opposite of "going your own ways, serving your own interests, or pursuing your own affairs" (58:13).

In the liturgical setting, Psalm 86 responds to this call by addressing the Lord in faith and penitence: "For you, O LORD, are good and forgiving, and great is your love toward all who call upon you" (5).

The calling of Levi by Jesus in today's Gospel is also a call to repentance. As a tax collector, Levi has almost certainly engaged in extortion, bribery, and corruption by which he has grown rich at the expense of others. Tax collectors worked for the Roman administration, and observant Jews regarded them as engaged in an inherently sinful occupation.

When Levi hears the call of Jesus, he rises and leaves his entire former way of life. He prepares a great feast in his house, emblematic of his conversion from a life of taking to a life of giving. Seeing this, the Pharisees and scribes complain that Jesus and his disciples eat and drink with tax collectors and sinners. Jesus responds: "Those who are well have no need of a physician, but those who are sick; I have come to call not the righteous but sinners to repentance" (Luke 5:31-32).

Disreputable characters though they may be, the one advantage the tax collectors have over the Pharisees and scribes is that they know their sickness and need of a physician—they know their sinfulness and their need for repentance.

Our Lord's message to the Pharisees and scribes is that since they believe themselves to be well, they have no need of him as their physician. Since they believe themselves to be righteous, repentance remains (for them) impossible.

As we begin Lent, the challenge for us is to truly discern whether we identify more with the tax collectors and sinners or the Pharisees and the scribes. To make the most of the Lenten season, we must acknowledge our need for repentance.

Monday in the First Week of Lent

Leviticus 19:1-2, 11-18
Psalm 19:7-14
Matthew 25:31-46

The Eucharistic readings for the first week in Lent explore what it means to follow Christ by resisting temptation and walking in the way of holiness. Today's readings from Leviticus and Matthew complement each other in a particularly challenging way.

The Leviticus reading calls the children of Israel to the imitation of God. Because God is holy, they are to be holy. A series of commandments follows, providing concrete illustrations of this principle. Most of these commandments prohibit social injustice and oppression: "You shall not defraud your neighbor; you shall not steal; and you shall not keep for yourself the wages of a laborer until morning" (19:13).

Four times, at the conclusion of each set of commandments, comes the ringing proclamation, "I am the LORD." The people are called to practice justice and righteousness precisely to reflect God's holiness in their corporate life. The issue is not so much what kind of people they are called to be as what kind of God has chosen them as his own. By obeying God's commandments, they reflect God's own character.

As Christians, we describe the kind of God we believe in as much by our deeds as by our words. If we're arrogant, unjust, or cruel in our dealings, we are, in effect, telling the world that we believe in an arrogant, unjust, and cruel God, no matter what else we may say about him. All too often the world has received precisely that message from the behavior of those who profess to be Christians.

The reading from Leviticus concludes with the commandment that sums up how best to witness to God's compassion and loving kindness: "You shall not take vengeance or bear a grudge against any of your people, but you shall love your neighbor as yourself: I am the LORD" (19:18).

This call to imitate and identify with God's holiness is only half the picture. The Gospel reading from Matthew, containing the famous parable of the sheep and the goats, supplies the other half. In Christ, God identifies with us, and particularly with "the least of these."

This parable sounds a dire and sobering warning. When we fail to care for those who are hungry, thirsty, strangers, naked, and sick, we not only betray our calling to be holy as the Lord God is holy, but we also neglect and mistreat the same God who, in the Incarnation, identifies himself with the poorest of the poor. "Truly I tell you, just as you did it to one of the least of these who are members of my family, you did it to me" (Matthew 25:40b).

The good news here is what Anglican theologian and historian A.M. Allchin called "the reciprocity of the divine and human" in Jesus Christ. Ultimately, all our attempts to identify with God and to realize God's holiness and righteousness are futile unless God first identifies with us. But in Christ God has identified with us, making it possible for us to do all that God commands.

So, it is Christ-in-us who ministers to Christ in "the least of these." In Christ, God infuses his holiness into fallen human nature, healing, restoring, and enabling it to fulfill God's command: "You shall be holy, for I the LORD your God am holy" (Leviticus 19:2b).

Tuesday in the First Week of Lent

Isaiah 55:6-11
Psalm 34:15-22
Matthew 6:7-15

The Lenten call to conversion is a call to prayer. The prophet Isaiah proclaims: "Seek the LORD while he may be found; call upon him while he is near" (Isaiah 55:1). The psalmist similarly emphasizes the efficacy of prayer: "The eyes of the LORD are upon the righteous, and his ears are open to their cry" (34:15).

In the Gospel reading, taken from the Sermon on the Mount, Jesus introduces the prayer we know as the Lord's Prayer or the Our Father. Initially, he warns those listening, "When you are praying, do not heap up empty phrases as the Gentiles do; for they think that they will be heard because of their many words" (6:7).

Exponents of what is known as "simple prayer from the heart" sometimes cite this verse to condemn repetitive prayers such as the Rosary or the Jesus Prayer. They dismiss what they call "canned prayers" and advocate simply telling God whatever is on our minds in our own words. While extemporaneous prayer is an important component of Christian spiritual life, nonetheless Jesus is teaching a formulaic prayer that can be used repetitively.

When Jesus says, "Do not heap up empty phrases as the Gentiles do, for they think that they will be heard for their many words," he is referring to petitions and intercessions addressed to the pagan gods and goddesses of the Roman pantheon. These deities were capricious beings, largely unconcerned with human affairs. The operating assumption governing classical Greek and Roman piety was that the gods needed to be flattered, cajoled, and manipulated into granting favors to human beings by elegant, wordy prayers.

The prayer Jesus teaches us to pray is built on a radically different foundation. Unlike the pagan deities who need to be told the worshipers' needs and wants, our heavenly Father knows what we need before we ask. The purpose of prayer is not to manipulate God through flattery into doing our will but rather to conform our wills to his. As Isaiah reminds us in the Old Testament reading:

> For my thoughts are not your thoughts,
>   nor are your ways my ways, says the LORD.
> For as the heavens are higher than the earth,
>   so are my ways higher than your ways
>   and my thoughts than your thoughts (55:8-9).

The unifying theme of the Lord's Prayer is the coming of God's kingdom. The petitions in this prayer ask God to give us those things we need to do his will on earth as it is done in heaven. And to be ready for the kingdom, we ask for our daily bread, the forgiveness of our sins, the grace to forgive others, escape from temptation, and deliverance from evil.

Lent is a time to practice praying as our Lord has taught us. The Lord's Prayer teaches us how to pray, and we cannot pray it too often. In the traditional curriculum of Christian catechesis, it is one of the four primary texts used for instruction in the faith, along with the Apostles' Creed, the Ten Commandments, and the Seven Sacraments. As Christians, we are called to pray, seeking above all else to do God's will and to be ready for the coming of God's kingdom.

Wednesday in the
First Week of Lent

Jonah 3:1-10
Psalm 51:11-18
Luke 11:29-32

Our Lord challenges his contemporaries in today's Gospel reading from Luke, calling them an evil generation seeking a sign. But the only sign given them will be the sign of Jonah, whose preaching spurred the inhabitants of Nineveh to repent. We find this story in today's Old Testament reading.

A curious feature of Jonah's preaching to the people of Nineveh is that he doesn't explicitly tell them to do anything. His message is simply, "Forty days, and Nineveh shall be overthrown" (3:4b). In the rest of the Book of Jonah, it becomes clear that he doesn't particularly want them to repent, and he's enormously disappointed when they do, because he'd much rather see God destroy them. But that's another story.

Despite Jonah's lackluster intention and efforts, his message carries an implicit invitation and promise, which the king of Nineveh recognizes. If all the inhabitants of the city repent and turn from their evil ways, then God may yet relent and turn from his fierce anger, so that Nineveh will not perish.

In response, the people not only forsake their evil ways—that alone would constitute repentance—but they also fast, dressing themselves in sackcloth and ashes, the adornment of those in deepest mourning. This fasting with sackcloth and ashes is not the *substance* but rather the *sign* of their repentance: their outward and visible expression of sorrow for their sins and supplication for God's mercy.

If the Ninevites had fasted and put on sackcloth and ashes but had not turned from their evil ways, it's not clear whether God would have spared them destruction. Repentance requires a visible and visceral change in how we live, an actual turning away from sin toward God, in which our hearts and minds are engaged to the depths of our being. The inner reality of repentance is effectually expressed in precisely such outward and explicit signs of humility and contrition as fasting with sackcloth and ashes.

In the Gospel reading, Jesus says that the inhabitants of Nineveh will rise at the last judgment and condemn the present generation for its lack of repentance in response to preaching far surpassing that of Jonah. Similarly, the Queen of the South (also known as the Queen of Sheba), who came from the ends of the earth to hear the wise counsel of King Solomon, will rise at the last judgment and condemn the present generation for its failure to listen to a wisdom far surpassing that of Solomon.

The sign of Jonah is a challenge to us in our own time. On the last day, when we are awakened from our sleep and summoned to judgment, what will the inhabitants of Nineveh say to us? Have we repented as they did? What will the Queen of the South say to us? Have we attended to God's wisdom as she did? Lent affords us the opportunity to ready ourselves to meet the inhabitants of Nineveh and the Queen of the South.

The ashes we received a week ago on Ash Wednesday were signs of repentance. As we continue our Lenten journey, we remember that our various disciplines of self-denial are no substitute for inner repentance and conversion. But they are signs of repentance—tokens of our intention to turn to God and forsake our sins. And to the extent that they help us do so, they make Lent a joyful time of spiritual refreshment and renewal.

Thursday in the First Week of Lent

Esther 14:1-6, 12-14
Psalm 138
Matthew 7:7-12

"Ask, and it will be given you; search, and you will find; knock, and the door will be opened to you" (Matthew 7:7). This is how Jesus teaches his disciples (and us) to persevere in prayer.

Today's reading from Esther offers an object lesson on the power of prayer. Esther is a beautiful, young Jewish woman and the new queen of Persia, having won a kingdom-wide contest judged by King Xerxes. Her identity as a Jew remains unknown to the king. A deadly threat to the Jewish people emerges in the person of the prime minister, Haman. He has taken offense at the refusal of the Jew Mordecai (who is also Esther's uncle and guardian) to bow down to him at the palace gates. In revenge for Mordecai's refusal to render obeisance, Haman persuades the king not only to have Mordecai hanged but also to kill all the Jews in Persia.

When Esther learns of Haman's plot, she conceives a plan to save her people. But first, she prays to the God of

Israel for assistance. Today's reading recounts her prayer, which combines penitence, petition, and intercession. She does not presume on Israel's special status as God's chosen people. On the contrary, she humbles herself before the Lord with dung and ashes, confessing that the people's sins have induced God to deliver them into the hands of their enemies. Nonetheless, she asks God to give her courage and eloquent speech, and she prays that God may turn the king's heart. She casts all her reliance on God.

Ultimately, Esther succeeds in saving her people. Haman is disgraced and hanged on the same gallows he had erected for Mordecai. Her subsequent prayer of thanksgiving might well have taken the form of the verse from today's psalm: "When I called, you answered me; you increased my strength within me" (138:4).

In today's Gospel, Jesus sets this dynamic of prayer and answer, of request and response, within the context of a loving parent-child relationship. "What man of you, if his son asks him for bread, will give him a stone? Or if he asks for a fish will give him a serpent?" His words take the form of an *a fortiori* argument: "If you then, who are evil, know how to give good gifts to your children, how much more will your Father in heaven give good things to those who ask him!"

But the obverse corollary is also implied: If God denies what we ask, that refusal must also be understood as the response of a loving father who truly knows what is in our best interests, seen from the perspective of eternity. If we ask for stones, it just may be that God will give us bread or, if we ask for a serpent, a fish.

Friday in the First Week of Lent

Ezekiel 18:21-28
Psalm 130
Matthew 5:20-26

In the service of the Jewish synagogue to the present day, a reading from one of the prophets follows the reading of the Torah—the Law. The reason for structuring the reading of scripture in this way is to understand both the letter and the spirit of the Law. Neither without the other is sufficient. The reading from the Torah gives the letter; the reading from the prophetic texts gives the spirit. To put it another way, the Torah provides the bones of the law, but the prophets give them breath.

A similar corollary is at work in today's Gospel lesson from Matthew. Here, in the Sermon on the Mount, Our Lord introduces the letter of the Law with the phrase: "You have heard that it was said to those of ancient times…" (5:21a). And then he introduces his interpretation of the spirit of the Law with the words, "But I say to you…"

Jesus' criticism of the scribes and Pharisees is that they pay too much attention to the letter and not enough to the spirit. This criticism undergirds his statement,

"For I tell you, unless your righteousness exceeds that of the scribes and Pharisees, you will never enter the kingdom of heaven" (5:20). The letter of the Law is concerned primarily with outward actions and their legal consequences: "Whoever murders shall be liable to judgment" (5:21b). But the spirit of the Law is concerned more with inward motivations and dispositions: "But I say to you that if you are angry with a brother or sister, you will be liable to judgment" (5:22a).

One temptation we face during Lent is focusing too much on the letter of the Law. No matter what we give up in the way of fasting, abstinence, and self-denial, and no matter what we take on in the way of extra devotion, study, or service, we must remember that the call to repentance and conversion is addressed first to the human heart.

Important as it is to do our best to adhere to the letter of our Lenten disciplines, we miss the point on a grand scale if we remain focused on the legalistic fulfillment of outward observances. Our Lord calls us to a deeper righteousness that consists of loving him with all our heart, mind, and will. And we shall keep a good Lent if our outward observances truly reflect such an interior turning to God.

Saturday in the First Week of Lent

Deuteronomy 26:16-19
Psalm 119:1-8
Matthew 5:43-48

Today's readings conclude the first full week of Lent with reflections on the place of law in God's relationship with his people. In the Bible, God never gives laws merely for their own sake. Instead, the Law's standards of moral, ritual, and civic behavior serve as a sign of the special relationship between the God who gives them and the people who receive and obey them.

In his speech to the Israelites in today's reading from Deuteronomy, Moses describes the covenant into which God and the people have entered. On one hand, the Lord has agreed to be their God. On the other hand, the people have agreed to be "a people holy to the Lord" (26:19b). That phrase means they are set apart as God's own special possession among all the peoples of the earth. The effective sign of both sides of this agreement is precisely the people's obedience: "to walk in his ways, to keep his statutes, his commandments, and his ordinances, and to obey him" (26:17b).

The Old Testament's emphasis on God's Law is never about obedience for the sake of obedience or rules for the sake of rules. Psalm 119 takes the form of an extended meditation on the joy of the Law. The psalmist uses the poetic device known as Hebrew parallelism to make it clear that obedience to the Law and a deeper relationship with God are interchangeable: "Happy are they who observe his decrees and seek him with all their hearts!" (119:2).

It follows that the relationship becomes distorted when mere outward conformity to God's decrees substitutes for the inward relationship they are meant to express. Jesus addresses this problem in today's Gospel. The point of the antitheses in the Sermon on the Mount—the sayings that follow the formula, "You have heard it said...but I say to you..."—is that an inward relationship with God takes us beyond merely obeying God's commandments.

So, we go beyond the commandment of loving our neighbor by loving our enemy as well, to be children of our Father in heaven, who "makes his sun rise on the evil and on the good, and sends rain on the righteous and on the unrighteous" (5:45). The point, ultimately, is not which commandments we are or are not obeying but rather how we are expressing and realizing our identity as children of our Father in heaven.

"Be perfect," Jesus concludes, "as your heavenly Father is perfect" (5:48). Here, the word "perfect" refers not so much to an unrealizable ideal of moral flawlessness as to a state of completion and wholeness. It means growing into such a close loving relationship with God that we instinctively see and respond to the world as he does. In this way, we fulfill our calling to be "a people holy to the LORD" (Deuteronomy 26:19b).

Monday in the Second Week of Lent

Daniel 9:3-10
Psalm 79:1-9
Luke 6:27-38

The destruction of Jerusalem and Solomon's Temple by the Babylonians in 586 BCE sets the scene for today's readings from Daniel and Psalm 79. The psalmist describes the horror of the scene in vivid language:

O God, the heathen have come into
        your inheritance;
they have profaned your holy temple;
    they have made Jerusalem a heap of rubble.
They have given the bodies of your servants
        as food for the birds of the air,
    and the flesh of your faithful ones to
        the beasts of the field.
They have shed their blood like water on
        every side of Jerusalem,
    and there was no one to bury them (79:1-3).

In different ways, the psalmist and Daniel confess that this catastrophe has come upon Jerusalem for the sins

36

of the people. Their only alternatives would be to blame God for capriciously delivering his people into the hands of their enemies or to conclude that God was powerless to prevent the people's defeat.

Both Daniel and the psalmist discern that the people's sins have brought this disaster down upon their own heads. Thus Daniel's prayer contrasts God's steadfast love and righteousness with the people's sin, rebellion, wickedness, and treachery.

Verse 9 presents an interesting question of interpretation. The King James Version reads: "To the LORD our God belong mercies and forgivenesses, *though* we have rebelled against him." This translation implies that despite our disobedience, God nonetheless remains merciful and forgiving, so that we have grounds for hope. Other translations use "for" instead of "though." "To the Lord our God belong mercy and forgiveness, *for* we have rebelled against him" (NRSV). This translation suggests that since we have rebelled against God, it is now God's prerogative to decide whether or not to exercise mercy and forgiveness. Precisely because we have sinned and forfeited any claim of our own, mercy and forgiveness are God's gifts to bestow or withhold as he pleases.

This latter translation reveals an essential quality of mercy. This word is often misused in our legal system, when in the sentencing phase of trials juries assess mitigating factors indicating that even though the accused has been found guilty, some degree of lenience in sentencing may be called for. However, merited lenience is not mercy at all.

Strictly speaking, mercy entails withholding or moderating punishment that the guilty party fully deserves. One can never earn, deserve, or merit mercy; it is by definition unearned, undeserved, and unmerited. Otherwise, it is not mercy but justice. When the Bible repeatedly describes God as merciful, it is asserting that God does not punish as we deserve but rather forgives. Our hope rests not in divine justice but in divine mercy.

Ironically, the psalmist prays in almost the same breath for God's mercy upon Israel and for God's vengeance upon Israel's enemies: "Pour out your wrath upon the heathen who have not known you and upon the kingdoms that have not called upon your Name" (79:6). In the Gospel, however, Jesus exhorts us to be merciful even as our heavenly Father is merciful. "Do not judge, and you will not be judged; do not condemn, and you will not be condemned. Forgive and you will be forgiven" (Luke 6:37).

Mercy and forgiveness are God's to bestow or withhold as he pleases. We have no claim on God's mercy; otherwise it would not be mercy. Jesus teaches repeatedly that we will be the recipients of God's mercy, insofar as we extend mercy to those who have wronged us and so prove ourselves to be children of our Father in heaven.

Tuesday in the Second Week of Lent

Isaiah 1:2-4, 16-20
Psalm 50:7-15, 22-24
Matthew 23:1-12

"Call no one your father on earth, for you have one Father—the one in heaven" (Matthew 23:9). This is a proof text invoked by many Protestants against a common Roman Catholic and Anglican form of address for men in holy orders. Parishioners regularly refer to male clergy as "Father," and many make it clear that they would be uncomfortable calling them anything else. But what does Jesus really mean in this instance?

This saying comes as the second of three exhortations. The first is, "You are not to be called rabbi, for you have one teacher, and you are all students" (23:8). And the third is, "Nor are you to be called instructors, for you have one instructor, the Messiah" (23:10). Rabbi, father, and instructor: Why does our Lord want his disciples not to address one another by these words?

The first and third terms may be taken together. In Judaism as it was practiced during Jesus' lifetime, the words rabbi and instructor both meant teacher: specifically, a teacher qualified to interpret the scriptures and adjudicate God's law. Being addressed as rabbi in this manner is a high honor, and Jesus doesn't want his disciples striving for such recognition. Jesus has just denounced the Jewish religious authorities for loving the places of honor at community festivities and assuming the best seats in the synagogue. Such self-aggrandizement has no place in the life of Jesus or in the lives of his disciples.

Another problem is that teachers tend to attract students. In the Judaism of Jesus' time, different schools followed the teachings of different rabbis, such as Shammai and Hillel. Jesus doesn't want to see the formation of such rivalries among his disciples. The one true teacher is Jesus himself, and his disciples mustn't jeopardize their unity by dividing into factions.

Jesus is teaching a similar lesson when he says, "Call no one your father on earth" (23:9a). The literal wording in the Greek is, "Do not call your earthly father," which probably means something like "Do not invoke your earthly father." Jesus is saying something much more radical than merely telling his disciples not to use the term "father" as a title of respect and honor. Rather, he is forbidding them to claim privilege within the Church on the basis of earthly parentage.

In other words, don't seek advantage over your fellow Christians by invoking your ancestry or your family name. The Church is called to be an egalitarian community in which worldly social distinctions based on race, class, education, or ethnicity have no place. No matter who your earthly parents may be, by baptism you have become a member of a new family in which all are called to treat one another as brothers and sisters, sons and daughters of the same Father in heaven.

Rabbi, father, instructor: The common theme running through Jesus' exhortation to avoid such terms is Christian unity. Being called rabbi or teacher tends to divide the Church into rival schools. Invoking the names of earthly fathers similarly tends to introduce divisions based on family status and social class.

This Gospel challenges us to ask how far we have allowed such distinctions to impede our unity with our fellow Christians. Within the Church, we are all family. We're called to treat our fellow Christians not just as co-religionists but also as veritable brothers and sisters in Christ.

Wednesday in the
Second Week of Lent

Jeremiah 18:1-11, 18-20
Psalm 31:9-16
Matthew 20:17-28

One of the most difficult challenges of the Christian life is forgiveness. Today's readings address this theme.

The prophet Jeremiah receives directions to speak prophetically to the inhabitants of Judah and Jerusalem, telling them to repent and return from their evil ways. Just as a potter will give up on a pot that fails to take proper shape, reworking it into another vessel, so the Lord can give up on a nation that does evil in his sight and build up another nation that will turn from evil and do good. Judah and Jerusalem must not presume on their special relationship with the LORD, who says: "Look, I am a potter shaping evil against you and devising a plan against you. Turn now, all of you from your evil way, and amend your ways and your doings" (Jeremiah 18:11b).

Instead of heeding Jeremiah, Judah and Jerusalem reject his message and plot against him. Overconfidently assessing their standing in God's sight, they boast: "for instruction shall not perish from the priest, nor counsel from the wise, nor the word from the prophet" (18:18a). The reading closes with Jeremiah's prayer: "Remember how I stood before you to speak good for them, to turn away your wrath from them" (18:20b).

Instead of calling down divine vengeance upon his persecutors, Jeremiah seeks the repentance and salvation of the children of Israel. Even as he suffers at the hands of Judah and Jerusalem, he calls upon the Lord to spare his tormentors.

In today's Gospel, Jesus enunciates a similar principle. In response to the request of the mother of James and John that her sons sit at his right and left hands in his kingdom, Jesus reminds the disciples, "Whoever wishes to be great among you must be your servant, and whoever wishes to be first among you must be your slave; just as the Son of Man came not to be served but to serve, and to give his life a ransom for many" (Matthew 20:26b-28).

Jesus knows that, like Jeremiah, he will be rejected and suffer at the hands of those to whom he has been sent. Yet his response is not to call down God's wrath upon his enemies. Rather, he understands his coming death as having precisely the opposite effect: to be a ransom for many—the means by which sin is forgiven and sinners reconciled to God.

It is important to be clear about what forgiveness does and does not mean. When others mistreat us, we are not called simply to take it. We have the right to use all legitimate means to protect ourselves, including in some cases seeing that those who have wronged us are held legally accountable for their actions. No one is suggesting that people who suffer violence or abuse should refrain from calling the police and pressing charges as appropriate.

What, then, about turning the other cheek? What is forgiveness? As Christians we *are* called to forgive, precisely by asking God to forgive those who have wronged or harmed us. Nothing is more destructive to our souls than resentment and bitterness. God intends good for all; the challenge is to ask God to bring even those who have mistreated us to the good he intended for them when he created them. Jeremiah and Jesus set the example. As we think about what we have given up for Lent, we need to remember that for our souls' health, one of the most important things we can ever give up is a grudge.

Thursday in the Second Week of Lent

Jeremiah 17:5-10
Psalm 1
Luke 16:19-31

To appreciate the full impact of today's Gospel story about the rich man and Lazarus, we need to try to hear it with the ears of its original audience. This parable tells of a reversal of fortunes so unexpected that it would have been shocking and scandalous to those hearing it for the first time.

In the beginning of the story, the rich man has an overabundance of wealth. He feasts extravagantly every day. Poor Lazarus sits outside the rich man's gate, hungry and lonesome, with the dogs licking his festering sores.

Lazarus's sores do not merely signify squalid living conditions. According to the Jewish Law, they make Lazarus ritually unclean. He is not allowed to enter either the Temple or a synagogue. Dogs are likewise considered unclean. So, the dogs licking his sores compound his status as a religious and social outcast—adding insult to injury.

To a first-century Jewish audience, it would have seemed obvious that God had blessed the rich man and cursed the poor man. The immediate assumption would have been that God was punishing Lazarus for his sins and blessing the rich man for his righteousness—indeed, the rich man and Lazarus were both receiving their just desserts.

The great reversal of fortunes takes place when the rich man and Lazarus die. Against all expectations, Lazarus turns out to be the one blessed by God, taken to the very bosom of Father Abraham, while the rich man turns out to be the one cursed by God, broiling in the unquenchable fire. All the social and political constructs of their earthly lives are turned inside out. A great, wide chasm replaces the gate that kept Lazarus and the rich man separated. Now, Lazarus is comforted, and the rich man is afflicted.

New Testament scholar N.T. Wright suggests that our Lord's primary aim in this parable is not to offer a description of the afterlife or to teach us how to go to heaven when we die. Rather, as in so many of the other parables, Jesus is illuminating the meaning of his own ministry.

At this point in Luke's Gospel, Jesus' critics have been complaining that he "welcomes sinners and eats with them." In this context, Lazarus stands as proxy for the outcasts with whom Jesus has been eating and drinking. The rich man represents the rich and powerful establishment types who consider themselves vastly superior to such notorious criminals and strange folk. The heavenly fellowship between Abraham and Lazarus represents the very earthy fellowship Jesus celebrates with the poor and marginalized of his own society. By rejecting Jesus, the rich and powerful place themselves on the far side of a great chasm that separates them from the ultimate reality of the kingdom of God.

The rich man just doesn't understand how the worm has turned so abruptly. He tries to ingratiate himself by addressing Abraham as "father." Worse, he still views Lazarus as a social inferior obligated to fetch a rich man a drink. When Abraham points out the great chasm separating them, the rich man asks for Lazarus to be sent to warn his five brothers of the punishment awaiting them if they don't mend their ways.

Abraham points out that the rich man's brothers have Moses and the prophets to guide them. The rich man could have avoided his fate by obeying the Torah's mandates to be generous and compassionate, to give alms and relieve the needs of the poor. And if the rich man's five brothers have been so preoccupied with their own lives that they have not listened to Moses and the prophets, then neither will they listen if someone should return to them from the dead.

Luke includes this last, stinging remark as a warning to all of us. As Christians, we have not only Moses and the prophets but also Jesus Christ who has returned from the dead. This parable warns us to open our hearts—to God and to all the Lazaruses who sit outside our gates.

Friday in the Second Week of Lent

Genesis 37:3-4, 12-28
Psalm 105:16-22
Matthew 21:33-43

Through the centuries, the Church has discerned that certain stories in the Hebrew scriptures anticipate and foreshadow the coming of Jesus Christ and God's ultimate plan for salvation. Biblical typology refers to a way of seeing how a story, image, person, place, or other element found in an Old Testament passage prefigures or foreshadows Christ and his saving grace for all people, as found in the New Testament. In biblical typology, the Old Testament element is called the type, and its New Testament fulfillment is called the antitype. The suffering of Joseph, in today's reading from Genesis, can function as a biblical type of the suffering of Christ.

As the beloved son of his father Israel (Jacob), Joseph points toward Jesus, beloved Son of God the Father. Both Joseph and Jesus suffer betrayal by those closest to them. Joseph's brothers sell him to traders from Midian for twenty shekels of silver; one of Jesus' disciples betrays him for thirty pieces of silver. Just as Joseph suffers the metaphorical death of descending into bondage and slavery in Egypt, so too does Jesus suffer the literal death of crucifixion and descent into hell.

The similarities don't end there. Twenty years later, Joseph has risen to become Pharaoh's chief minister. When his brothers go down to Egypt in search of food during a great famine, they initially don't recognize Joseph as their brother, but at length he reveals himself to them. They are rightly terrified, thinking that now they will receive their just desserts. But, contrary to all expectations, Joseph forgives them. Here is an anticipation of Christ's resurrection: Joseph (mistakenly thought to be dead by his brothers) reveals himself as the source of their life and the agent of their deliverance from certain death.

Often, the key figures and events in stories told by Jesus point toward his coming death and resurrection. In today's Gospel, set in the precincts of the Temple in Jerusalem, Jesus tells the parable of the wicked tenants. He has just cleansed the Temple of the moneychangers— overturning their tables and driving out the stockmen who sold animals for the ritual sacrifices. The chief priests and elders have demanded to know under whose authority Jesus performs such actions. The parable is part of his answer to the questions they pose.

When Jesus finishes the story of the tenants killing the landlord's beloved son, he asks the chief priests and elders to supply their own ending: When the owner of the vineyard comes, what will he do to the tenants? The chief priests and elders burst out, righteously indignant: "He will put those wretches to a miserable death, and lease the vineyard to other tenants who will give him the produce at the harvest time" (Matthew 21:41).

In response, Jesus cryptically quotes a psalm speaking of a stone that is initially rejected by the builders but then somehow becomes the building's chief cornerstone. Then, addressing the priests and elders directly, Jesus concludes: "Therefore I tell you, the kingdom of God will be taken away from you and given to a people that produces the fruits of the kingdom" (Matthew 21:43).

As authority figures, the chief priests and elders have naturally identified with the landlord as the protagonist in the story. Now, with a shock, they realize that all along Jesus has been casting them as the wicked tenants! The symbolism is transparent. The landlord is God; the vineyard is Israel; the messengers are God's prophets; and the landowner's son is Jesus himself. The son is cast out of the vineyard and killed, clearly prefiguring Jesus taken outside the walls of Jerusalem and crucified.

N.T. Wright, the New Testament scholar, points out that Jesus' comment about a rejected stone becoming the chief cornerstone comes into focus when we realize that the Hebrew word for stone, *eben*, closely resembles the word for son, *ben*. Jesus is saying that his rejection and death will not be the end; somehow he will return and become the foundation of a new spiritual edifice that will replace the present temple made of stone. On that day, even those who cast him out and killed him will have the opportunity—just like Joseph's brothers—to repent of their sin and recognize Jesus as the source of their life and salvation.

From the beginning, the scriptures present a constantly repeating pattern of death and resurrection, redemption and salvation. The story that God has been telling all along finds its fulfillment in Jesus Christ, but is anticipated in countless ways beforehand, and is being lived out in countless ways, until the great last day.

Saturday in the
Second Week of Lent

Micah 7:14-15, 18-20
Psalm 103:1-4(5-8)9-12
Luke 15:11-32

In a parish I once attended before I went to seminary, a certain woman (we will call her Mildred) had a real problem with today's story from Luke. Mildred was the archetypal church lady—she attended Sunday services without fail and Wednesday evenings, too; she sang in the choir, cooked for the parish suppers, and supported all the church's events.

Mildred was a dear soul—faithful and devout. But she had a hard time with three stories in particular. The first was the parable of the laborers in the vineyard, where those who arrive at four in the afternoon receive the same wages as those who've been working since eight in the morning. The second was the story of Mary and Martha. Mildred frankly thought Martha was completely justified in her complaint about Mary not helping in the kitchen. And thirdly, Mildred really had a problem with the Prodigal Son. Mildred found the father in the story totally unfair and identified completely with the resentments expressed by the older brother. She couldn't understand why Jesus would tell a parable exalting such unfairness. These stories frankly made Mildred angry with Jesus.

Mildred was no hypocrite. She resented (and complained bitterly) when she saw other people who hadn't been around the parish nearly as long as she had or folks she thought didn't work nearly as hard as she did being given positions of leadership on parish committees—or simply receiving (what she considered) a disproportionate share of the rector's attention.

Now, as contrarian as Mildred's reactions were—and they were wrongheaded—I will say one thing in her defense: Mildred had a clear appreciation of the challenge of these Gospel stories. Struggling as she did with these stories, Mildred had an advantage over many of us, for whom the greater danger is complacency. The teachings of Jesus are not always comforting or reassuring. They do not always reinforce our preconceived worldview. Many of the parables are especially subversive of the world's assumptions and values.

If we don't find the parables challenging, maybe even disorienting and unsettling, we are not really listening. The good news for Mildred (and for us, when we find ourselves in her shoes) was that she *was* hearing them— and finding them appropriately disturbing.

Another name for the parable of the Prodigal Son is the parable of the Jealous Older Brother. The older brother's problem in the story is a combination of two things: blindness to his own gifts and an unwarranted posture of chronic self-righteousness. One of the consequences of our fallen condition is a tendency to become envious of those who have more in the way of material wealth than we do while at the same time feeling morally superior to them. They may be richer than we are, but we're better people. In this way, we develop attitudes of jealousy and disdain simultaneously.

These attitudes prevent the cultivation of two virtues that are completely necessary to any healthy relationship with God: gratitude for the gifts we have received and sorrow for our sins. The older brother's spiritual predicament is that he's so jealous of the special treatment given to the prodigal that he forgets to be thankful for his own privileged position in the family. And he's so full of righteous indignation at the prodigal's loose living that he can't recognize his own sinfulness.

The father's words to his oldest son are really an admonition to stop taking himself so seriously. There's a party going on! As Episcopal priest and author Robert Farrar Capon recasts it: "Go inside, pour yourself a drink, have a good time, and stop being such a bore!" These are words of tough love that I suspect we all need to hear from time to time.

N.T. Wright points out that the parable's abrupt ending leaves the hearers hanging. Jesus leaves the ending open, knowing that we must supply the answer ourselves, with our own response to his invitation to join in the great feast of God's kingdom. The question is whether we'll stay outside and keep on making ourselves miserable, or go inside and join the party.

Alternative Proper for a Weekday in the Third Week of Lent

Exodus 17:1-7
Psalm 95:6-11
John 4:5-26 (27-38) 39-42

(NOTE: This proper repeats readings for the Third Sunday in Lent, Year A, and so is especially suitable for use in Years B and C. See explanation on page 4.)

Today's readings recall crises occasioned by a lack of water. Thirst is one of the most urgent physical longings we can experience. After leaving a portion of the Sinai referred to as The Desert of Sin, Moses and the Hebrews find themselves in a dry and wasted place called Rephidim. The people start grumbling: "Why did you bring us out of Egypt, to kill us and our children and livestock with thirst?" (Exodus 17:3b).

This moment represents a crisis of faith as well as a threat to physical life. Even after their miraculous escape from Egypt, the Israelites doubt that the Lord who delivered them from the hands of the Egyptians can also deliver them from dying of thirst in the wilderness.

Moses cries to the Lord, "What shall I do with this people? They are almost ready to stone me" (Exodus 17:4). The Lord tells Moses to strike the rock at a place called Horeb with his staff. When Moses does so, water gushes out, and the people are sated.

Providing water in the desert solves two problems at once. At the physical level, the people are saved from dehydration and death. At the spiritual level, God reaffirms both his presence with this community and his commitment to provide for the needs of the entire assembly wherever they go. Water streaming from the rock at Horeb becomes a sign not only of physical survival and life but also of God's providence and care.

In the reading from John's Gospel, we find Jesus traveling through Samaria. Wearied by his journey, he sits down by a well. When a Samaritan woman comes to draw water, a tired and thirsty Jesus asks her for a drink.

When this unnamed woman questions how it is that Jesus is transgressing all kinds of social and religious boundaries to ask her for a drink of water, he takes the conversation to a whole new level. "If you knew the gift of God, and who it is that is saying to you, 'Give me a drink,' you would have asked him and he would have given you living water" (4:10).

What follows is a wonderful dialogue of double meaning typical of John's Gospel. In ancient Palestine, living water meant the kind of water you get from a spring or a running stream: fresh, clear, flowing water, gurgling, bubbly, and vital—not like the murky, brackish water found stagnating in wells and cisterns.

When Jesus tells the woman that he can give her living water, it sounds like a pleasant alternative to what is in the well. "Sir, give me this water, so that I may never be thirsty or have to keep coming here to draw water" (4:15). She's probably being sarcastic, doubting that Jesus can give her such water, just as the children of Israel once doubted that God could provide water in a barren desert.

But Jesus isn't speaking of literal water: "Everyone who drinks of this water will be thirsty again, but those who drink of the water that I will give them will never be thirsty. The water that I will give will become in them a spring of water gushing up to eternal life" (4:13-14).

Jesus is speaking of a spiritual gift that only he can give. Just as our bodies thirst for water, so our spirits thirst for God. Jesus is saying he has come to quench the deepest thirst of our souls.

The Samaritan woman goes into the city and says to the people, "Come, and see a man who told me everything I have ever done! He cannot be the Messiah, can he?" (4:29).

Clearly, she has received the living water that Jesus was offering her. She had doubted Jesus, just as the Israelites doubted Moses in the wilderness. But just as the Israelites ended up drinking water from the rock, so the Samaritan woman ended up drinking of God's Spirit.

At those times in our lives when we feel spiritually dry or even abandoned by God, we do well to remember the Israelites in the wilderness and the Samaritan woman at the well. They received a remedy for their thirst. Similarly, we trust God to quench our spiritual thirst with springs of living water, welling up to eternal life.

Monday in the Third Week of Lent

2 Kings 5:1-15b
Psalm 42:1-7
Luke 4:23-30

Both of today's readings describe what might be called misaligned expectations. When Naaman, the commander of the armies of the King of Syria, comes to the house of Elisha the prophet, he is sorely disappointed and enraged when the prophet sends a messenger instructing him that if he will bathe seven times in the River Jordan, his flesh will be restored and he will be made clean.

The prescribed remedy is not what Naaman expects. "I thought that for me he would surely come out, and stand and call upon the name of the LORD his God, and wave his hand over the spot, and cure the leprosy. Are not… the rivers of Damascus better than all the waters of Israel? Could I not wash in them, and be clean?" (2 Kings 5:11b-12). It seems that Naaman initially mistakes the prophet's instructions for a folk remedy having nothing to do with Israel's God. He wants the prophet to call upon the Lord. In this sense, he displays genuine faith. He didn't come all this way to bathe—he could have done that at home.

Nonetheless, Naaman dips himself seven times in the Jordan when his servants persuade him that he would surely have done something difficult had the prophet asked. Some commentators suggest that the waters of the Jordan are so muddy that no one would expect them to have healing powers, and Elisha sends Naaman to bathe in them to demonstrate that true healing comes neither from the prophet nor from the waters but from God alone. The point is not lost on Naaman, who returns to Elisha declaring, "Now I know that there is no God in all the earth except in Israel" (5:15).

Today's Gospel cites this episode to illustrate what Jesus means when he says that "no prophet is acceptable in his own country" (Revised Standard Version, 4:24). After reading to the townspeople of Nazareth from the scroll of the prophet Isaiah, Jesus discerns that they are inwardly grumbling that he should perform the same miracles of healing for them that he has performed in other places, such as Capernaum. After all, Nazareth is where he grew up: "Is this not Joseph's son?" In response, Jesus points out that his calling is to take his ministry out into the world beyond his hometown. The very familiarity of the people among whom he grew up would be too limiting.

Jesus cites the examples of the prophets Elijah and Elisha. There were many widows in Israel in the time of Elijah, but Elijah was sent only to a widow of Zarephath, in the land of Sidon. And there were many lepers in Israel in the time of Elisha, but the only one cleansed was Naaman the Syrian. In this instance, the misalignment of expectations goes unresolved. The townspeople of Nazareth take offense and attempt to kill Jesus. But, as Luke cryptically puts it, Jesus passes through the midst of the mob and continues on his way.

We need to be careful about our expectations of God, because often he does not do what we expect. The last thing Naaman was expecting was to be told to bathe seven times in the Jordan. The real test of his obedience was whether he was willing to follow simple instructions, rather than a difficult and elaborate scheme. Similarly, the townspeople of Nazareth were expecting dazzling displays of miraculous power from Jesus; all he wanted from them was simple attentiveness to his words.

During Lent, we may find that what really counts in growing closer to the Lord is nothing complicated or heroic: perseverance in the recitation of the Daily Office and attendance at the Eucharist; continuing fidelity to the basic practices of prayer, fasting, and almsgiving that constitute our Lenten rules.

We do well to keep it simple.

Tuesday in the Third Week of Lent

Song of the Three Young Men 2-4, 11-20a
(In some Bibles, Daniel 3:25-27, 34-43)
Psalm 25:3-10
Matthew 18:21-35

Some years ago, actress Susan Sarandon played Sister Helen Prejean in the movie, *Dead Man Walking*. The movie tells the story of a nun who becomes the spiritual advisor to a convicted murderer on death row, with a particular focus on the days leading up to his execution. One of the film's most dramatic moments depicts Sister Helen's encounter with the parents of the two young people murdered by the inmate. The parents of the victims desperately want the execution to go forward; their lives are consumed by a desire for retribution, for their understanding of justice to be served. Watching the film, our reaction might well be, "Who can blame them?" If we were in their position, would forgiveness be the first thing on our minds?

Forgiving those who have injured us is one of the most difficult demands of the gospels. Yet Jesus teaches us to pray, "Forgive us our trespasses, as we forgive those who trespass against us." The parable we find in today's Gospel embodies our Lord's teaching about forgiveness.

At the beginning of the reading, Peter asks how many times he must forgive someone for repeated offenses: Is seven times enough? In other words, doesn't there come a point when someone has hurt you one time too many, and you just can't forgive them again no matter how contrite or sorry they are?

Peter probably thinks he's being enormously generous in offering to forgive someone seven whole times. But Jesus says no, not seven times, do it seventy times seven—a biblical euphemism indicating an infinitely large number. For Christians, there must be no limit on the mandate to forgive those who sin against us.

We need to understand, however, what forgiveness is and isn't. When someone has hurt us, forgiveness does not mean saying, "Oh, that's all right; it doesn't matter." It's not all right, and it does matter. If it really were all right, there'd be nothing to forgive.

To seek forgiveness is to admit that one has done wrong. And to offer forgiveness does not excuse injury or insult. Instead, offering forgiveness means overcoming the instinct to strike back—it involves letting go of the desire for vengeance, retribution, or any compensation in response to hurt or harm.

Forgiveness does not mean that violent criminals should not be incarcerated. It does not mean that chief financial officers embezzling company funds should keep their jobs. It does not mean that injured spouses should continue to live in abusive marriages. It does not mean that the Church should cover up for priests who have molested children. In each of these situations, decisive steps are necessary to safeguard the community, to protect the innocent, and to hold people accountable for their wrong actions.

But even in these difficult and emotionally wrought situations, forgiveness does mean refusing to be ruled by hatred, malice, vindictiveness, and desire for retribution, which can consume us and poison our own attitudes and behavior. When we forgive, we refuse to let our lives and identities be defined by our injuries or those who have injured us.

The parable in today's Gospel illustrates the way to become people who forgive as we have been forgiven. A king releases a slave from a debt of ten thousand talents. But then that same slave refuses to forgive a debt of a hundred denarii owed to him by another slave.

The key to learning to forgive as we have been forgiven is to understand the substantive difference between the two slaves' debt burdens. A denarius was roughly equal to the day's wage of a laborer. But a talent was equivalent to

6,000 denarii. So, the ten thousand talents that the servant owed the king was an astronomical sum. There was no way that the servant could have paid off the debt. It cost the king infinitely more to forgive the debt owed by the servant than it would have cost the servant to forgive the debt owed by his fellow servant.

We find the motivation to forgive others when we realize the lengths to which God has gone in order to forgive us. Jesus died on the cross to forgive us our sins and reconcile us to God. It cost him far more to forgive us than it will ever cost us to forgive anyone else. So, to become forgiving people, we must keep our gaze fixed on the cross. Then, and only then, will we know the freedom and joy that comes from being able to forgive others as God has forgiven us.

Wednesday in the Third Week of Lent

Deuteronomy 4:1-2, 5-9
Psalm 78:1-6
Matthew 5:17-19

With our contemporary culture's emphasis on personal freedom, we tend not to think of laws, rules, and regulations as gifts. They may seem at best a necessary evil. But the Old Testament and Gospel readings for today depict God's commandments as among God's greatest gifts to his people.

Moses and Jesus both emphasize the need to remember and keep all of God's commandments, not just some of them. Moses declares that these statutes and ordinances must not be forgotten, so that the people will faithfully fulfill them from generation to generation and astound their neighbors with the depth of their wisdom. In particular: "You must neither add anything to what I command you nor take away anything from it, but keep the commandments of the LORD your God with which I am charging you" (Deuteronomy 4:2).

In our reading from Matthew's Gospel, Jesus sounds a similar note: "Do not think that I have come to abolish the law or the prophets; I have come not to abolish but to fulfill....Therefore, whoever breaks one of the least of these commandments, and teaches others to do the same, will be called least in the kingdom of heaven" (5:17, 19). The point here is that both Israel and the nascent Church have written records that reveal God's will for humanity. We are neither to add anything nor take anything away. Those being ordained in The Episcopal Church swear an oath containing the words: "I solemnly declare that I do believe the Holy Scriptures of the Old and New Testaments to be the Word of God, and to contain all things necessary to salvation" (*The Book of Common Prayer, 1979*, p. 526).

The reading of scripture shapes our lives together in the Church: from proclamations in the liturgy, to public commentary in the form of sermons, to Bible study in small groups or as individuals. Lent is traditionally a time when Christians rededicate themselves to reading, studying, and meditating upon God's Word.

This work of rededication, admittedly, is not always easy. Much of scripture is beautiful, instructive, and inspiring. But when the writer of Psalm 137 talks about dashing children's heads against rocks, I am upset and repelled. Yet the Church's conviction is that God has spoken in all of these stories, not just the ones that make us happy or feel good, and we believe the definitive record of his speech is contained in the canon of scripture—the whole canon, not just the bits we like. We are called to take the canon as it has been handed to us—we cannot relax or set aside those parts of scripture that elude, confuse, or offend us.

But when we are honest, we admit that we cannot set aside, ignore, or suppress our reactions of confusion, bewilderment, or repugnance, either. We are called to honor both the authority of the sacred text and our reactions to it. We must live in the tension of recognizing that even the difficult passages of scripture carry the authority of God's revelation, sometimes in ways and with words that we don't yet fully comprehend. We continue to read, study, meditate, and listen, confident that in the fullness of time all shall be made clear.

Thursday in the Third Week of Lent

Jeremiah 7:23-28
Psalm 95:6-11
Luke 11:14-23

Today's readings address what might be called "the problem of hard-heartedness." Every day at Morning Prayer during Lent, we are encouraged to read the longer version of the *Venite*, Psalm 95, which includes the lines:

> Today if ye will hear his voice, harden not
>   your hearts
>   as in the provocation,
>   and as in the day of temptation in the
>   wilderness,
> When your fathers tempted me,
>   proved me, and saw my works.
>   (*The Book of Common Prayer, 1979*, p. 146)

Throughout the Bible, God calls people into relationship, inviting them to follow him and walk in his ways. Many great figures in scripture (Noah and Abraham immediately come to mind) find their lives profoundly changed and fundamentally blessed when they accept God's invitation into a covenantal relationship.

Subsequently, when people stray from the commandments, God calls them to repentance, often by sending prophets to warn them of the consequences of their disobedience. The problem of hard-heartedness comes into play whenever people hear God's voice—either in the initial call to follow or in the subsequent call to repent—and instead of responding positively, they resist.

In today's reading from Jeremiah, God complains: "From the day that your ancestors came out of the land of Egypt until this day, I have persistently sent all my servants the prophets to them, day after day; yet they did not listen to me, or pay attention, but they stiffened their necks. They did worse than their ancestors did" (7:25-26). In biblical language, stiffening one's neck is the functional equivalent of hardening one's heart. Even though the prophets speak God's words, the people do not listen or obey.

The same sort of dynamic is at work in today's Gospel. Jesus is casting out demons—a sure sign of both the presence and power of the kingdom of God in his ministry. Some of the onlookers attribute his ability to cast out demons to Beelzebul, the prince of demons. Others seek from him a heavenly sign as their test of Jesus' divine authority. The problem is that once people have rejected the sign that he's already given—the casting out of demons—no further sign will be forthcoming nor would any such sign be convincing. The problem is one of spiritual blindness, not an actual lack of signs and wonders. This blindness is rooted in the people's hard-hearted refusal to acknowledge the signs Jesus has been showing them all along.

Key themes of Lent are listening and responding to the call to forsake hardness of heart. "Today if ye will hear his voice, harden not your hearts…" Our Lenten practices are worthwhile to the extent they help soften our hearts, disposing us to listen and respond affirmatively to God's call in Christ Jesus.

Friday in the Third Week of Lent

Hosea 14:1-9
Psalm 81:8-14
Mark 12:28-34

In today's Gospel from Mark, a scribe asks Jesus, "Which Commandment is the first of all?" It was a common question among the rabbis of the time: Of all the hundreds of commandments, which one stands first in importance as summing up and interpreting all the rest? Jesus responds with two proof texts directly from the Torah. First, he quotes Deuteronomy 6:4-5, "Hear, O Israel: The LORD is our God, the LORD alone. You shall love the LORD your God with all your heart, and with all your soul, and with all your might." To this, Jesus joins a second text from Leviticus 19:18b, "You shall love your neighbor as yourself: I am the LORD."

According to some commentators, Jesus' answer to the question about the most important commandment differs significantly from answers given by many religious authorities of that time. Some held that keeping the Sabbath was the most important commandment, while others maintained that the most important commandment was circumcision. Still others regarded making the appropriate sacrifices at the Temple as the most vital portion of the Law.

There were some teachers who gave answers similar to that of Jesus. Hillel the Elder, a well-regarded and much beloved rabbi during the first century BCE, once summed up the entire Torah for a Gentile who wanted to convert: "What is hateful to thee, do not do unto thy fellow man: this is the whole Law, the rest is commentary; go and learn." Akiva ben Joseph, another pillar of rabbinical exegesis in late antiquity, declared that the most important principle of Judaism was, "You shall love your neighbor as yourself."

The singular and unique genius of Jesus' response is marrying these two texts together. As a unit, these two commandments have become known as the Summary of the Law. In The Episcopal Church, we recite Matthew's version at the beginning of every celebration of the Holy Eucharist: Rite One.

The Summary of the Law furnishes the two headings under which the Christian tradition has arranged the Ten Commandments: Commandments One through Four tell us what it means to love God with all our heart, mind, and strength. Commandments Five through Ten explain what it means to love our neighbors as ourselves. Under the headings of each of the Ten Commandments, Christian ethicists have extrapolated many more principles, rules, and precepts of moral behavior. But they all fall under the wide umbrella of our Lord's Summary of the Law—love God and love your neighbor.

Very simply put, Christian discipleship isn't about obeying rules. It is about love—or, more precisely, about learning to love the right things in the right way.

John says, "God is love" (1 John 4:8). By his life, death, and resurrection, Christ reveals God's love for us. Christ alone perfectly fulfills his own commandments by loving God with all his heart, mind, soul, and strength—and by loving his neighbor as himself. As those baptized into Christ's Body—baptized into his death and resurrection—we are called to manifest Christ's life in the world by loving as he loves. In John's Gospel, Jesus commands us, "Just as I have loved you, you also should love one another" (13:34).

When we are trying to decide on the ethics of one course of action or another, a key question to ask is which action most fully expresses love of God and love of neighbor. This is a fairly simple, and very effective test.

The great genius of the Summary of the Law is the coupling of two commandments that really are inseparable. We cannot love God without loving our neighbor. After all, our neighbors have been made in God's image. John's first epistle puts it: "Those who say, 'I love God,' and hate their brothers or sisters, are liars; for those who do not love a brother or sister whom they have seen, cannot love God whom they have not seen" (1 John 4:20). But neither can we love our neighbor adequately without loving God. As Christians, we're not given the option of choosing one or the other. We are called to do both.

Saturday in the Third Week of Lent

Hosea 6:1-6
Psalm 51:15-20
Luke 18:9-14

The prophet Hosea subtly anticipates the contrast between the Pharisee and tax collector that we meet in the reading from Luke. As the Old Testament reading begins, we hear the voices of unidentified repentant sinners: "Come, let us return to the LORD; for it is he who has torn, and he will heal us; he has struck down, and he will bind us up" (6:1). The people praying to God in their distress have suffered affliction on account of sin and are turning to the Lord for forgiveness and healing.

In the second half of the reading from Hosea, God speaks not to the penitent sinners who have just spoken but to the rest of the inhabitants of Judah and Israel, asking them, "What shall I do with you, O Ephraim? What shall I do with you, O Judah? Your love is like a morning cloud, like the dew that goes away early" (6:4). This unflattering description stands in explicit contrast to the earlier portrayal of the Lord whose "appearing is as sure as the dawn" who "will come to us like the showers, like the spring rains that water the earth" (6:3).

The inhabitants of Judah and Israel are subject to divine judgment: "For I desire steadfast love and not sacrifice; the knowledge of God rather than burnt offerings" (6:6). The reading thus draws a contrast between repentant sinners returning to the Lord in supplication and humility, and those who outwardly observe religious formality without the knowledge of God or the practice of steadfast love.

The Pharisee and the tax collector in today's Gospel reading from Luke exemplify this stark contrast. The Pharisee is so full of religion that he has little room in his life for God. He begins his prayer on the right note, "God, I thank you…" But as he continues, the Pharisee's discourse is really all about himself. The tax collector, by contrast, is so convicted by his own sinfulness and unworthiness that he casts himself on God's mercy, not even lifting his eyes toward heaven but standing afar, beating his breast and pleading for forgiveness. According to Jesus, the tax collector, not the Pharisee, goes home justified—one who exalts himself will be humbled and one who humbles himself will be exalted.

By this point in our journey, we are most likely quite conscious of our successes and failures in keeping our Lenten disciplines. What goals did we set for ourselves in the days leading up to Shrove Tuesday and Ash Wednesday, three and a half weeks ago? How well are we keeping our disciplines?

Most likely, our records are mixed. Maybe we haven't been as successful in maintaining our disciplines as we would like. Perhaps we can begin to see Lent as a microcosm of the entire Christian experience. We try to follow in the way of discipleship, observing the practices that the Church offers us as means of growing in grace. But we will be more successful in some of these efforts than in others.

To the extent that we have done well in keeping our Lenten disciplines, our temptation may be to adopt the posture of the Pharisee, thanking God that we're not like those others who neglect to do what we do. A healthy dose of humility is always the antidote to becoming too proud of our spiritual achievements. If, on the other hand, we have fallen down in keeping our Lenten disciplines, it is not too late to say we're sorry, pick ourselves up, dust ourselves off, and start over again. This is as true in the Christian life in general as in the keeping of Lent in particular. It is never too late to repent.

Alternative Proper for a Weekday in the Fourth Week of Lent

Micah 7:7-9
Psalm 27:1, 10-18
John 9:1-13(14-27)28-38

(NOTE: This proper repeats the Gospel reading for the Fourth Sunday in Lent, Year A, and so is especially suitable for use in Years B and C.)

Lent has been described as a journey through deepening gloom, culminating in the near total darkness of Good Friday and exploding into brilliant light on Easter Day. Themes running through today's readings are the contrasts between light and darkness, between seeing and not seeing, between blindness and sight.

These contrasts dominate today's Gospel reading from John. The man born blind receives his sight in more ways than one. At the natural level, we witness a miraculous physical healing. Jesus makes a bit of mud and smears it across the man's eyes and tells him to go and wash in the pool of Siloam. When the blind man does so, his eyes are suddenly opened. Physically blind from birth, he receives the gift of sight.

At the same time, the blind man's eyes are opened spiritually as well. When he comes back home with his sight restored, people naturally want to know what happened. Each time the formerly blind man explains the story, he displays a little more understanding of who Jesus is.

The first time, talking to his neighbors, he describes his healer simply as "the man called Jesus" (9:11). Then, when the Pharisees ask him what he thinks of this man who has opened his eyes, he tells them that Jesus is "a prophet" (9:17). A little later, when the Pharisees try to convince him to denounce Jesus as a sinner for healing on the Sabbath, he refuses to do so, telling them, "If this man were not from God, he could do nothing" (9:33). Finally, when he meets Jesus again, he calls him "Lord," and falls down and worships him. He has received sight in both a physical sense and a spiritual sense—and he has come out of the darkness of unbelief into the light of faith.

This healing story conveys profound symbolism. When Jesus tells the blind man to go and wash in the pool, we see a clear and unmistakable image of baptism. Not only that, but also from the earliest days Christian baptism has included an anointing with holy oil (chrism), and in this story of the blind man, we have an anointing (of sorts), as well.

So, the healing of the man born blind is an allusion to Christian baptism. Symbolically, the story is telling us that the sacrament of baptism brings us out of the darkness of sin into the light of Christ's righteousness. The early Church often referred to baptism as "enlightenment" and to the newly baptized as "enlightened ones."

This past Sunday marked the mid-point of our journey through the gathering darkness of Lent toward the light of Easter. Lent originated as a time of preparation for baptism. During Lent, it's traditional to pray for those preparing to receive the sacrament of baptism, that they may persevere in the journey they have begun. And for those already baptized, this season similarly affords an opportunity to continue to learn daily what it means to walk in the light of the Lord.

Monday in the
Fourth Week of Lent

Isaiah 65:17-25
Psalm 30:1-6, 11-13
John 4:43-54

Yesterday, on Mid-Lent Sunday, we turned a corner in our Lenten journey. During the first three weeks of Lent, the daily Eucharistic readings have explored the meaning of repentance and its associated disciplines of prayer, fasting, and almsgiving.

From today through Holy Week, the Gospel readings are taken from John and chronicle the mounting tension between Jesus and the Jewish religious authorities, eventually resulting in Jesus' arrest and crucifixion. The readings for the next three weeks panoramically depict what it means to walk the Way of the Cross—by showing how Our Lord's obedience to his Father leads inexorably toward his Passion and death.

The synoptic gospels (Matthew, Mark, and Luke) depict the Way of the Cross in terms of the final journey of Jesus and his disciples to Jerusalem, following Peter's confession at Caesarea Philippi and the Transfiguration, to be in the holy city to celebrate Passover. John's version of these events mostly ignores the geographical journey so important to the other three gospel writers and instead develops a parallel theme with a series of signs and discourses in which the conflict between Jesus and those who oppose him becomes progressively more intractable.

Signs (in Greek, *semeia*) is John's word for Jesus' miracles. Matthew, Mark, and Luke generally refer to the miracles as *dynameis*, "acts of power," meant to demonstrate the nearness of the Kingdom of God. But for John, the signs have the purpose and intention of evoking faith in Jesus as God's Son, the Messiah. While these signs evoke deepened faith among Jesus' disciples, they often have the opposite effect on Jesus' opponents. They seem to stiffen and harden their opposition to him. Following each of the signs, the religious authorities typically question and challenge Jesus, who responds in turn by highlighting his claims about himself. The conflicts escalate.

Today's Gospel presents the second of Jesus' signs in John: the healing of a royal official's son who is at the point of death. (The first sign was changing water into wine at the wedding in Cana.) Apart from the passing remark, "Unless you see signs and wonders you will not believe" (4:48). Jesus does not hint at controversy or conflict. When the royal official pleads, "Sir, come down before my little boy dies" (4:49b), Jesus shows incredible compassion, performing the healing from a distance. The immediate result of this miracle is a conversion to faith in Jesus by the official and his entire household.

Today's reading from the prophet Isaiah envisions the coming reign of God. Isaiah foretells a time when "No more shall the sound of weeping be heard in [Jerusalem], or the cry of distress. No more shall there be in it an infant that lives but a few days, or an old person who does not live out a lifetime…They shall not labor in vain, or bear children for calamity; for they shall be offspring blessed by the LORD—and their descendants as well" (65:19b-20, 23).

Taken together, today's readings make a simple point. Even though their purpose is to evoke faith, Jesus' signs and wonders are nonetheless acts of compassion and kindness through which people experience healing, restoration, and wholeness. Jesus performs good works and delivers people from distress. The royal official in today's gospel reading could well have recited the words of today's psalm: "You have turned my wailing into dancing; you have put off my sack-cloth and clothed me with joy. Therefore my heart sings to you without ceasing; O LORD my God I will give you thanks for ever" (30:12-13).

In the Acts of the Apostles, Peter describes Jesus having gone about "doing good and healing all who were oppressed by the devil, for God was with him" (10:38). Later in John's Gospel, Jesus says to those who are about to stone him: "I have shown you many good works from the Father. For which of these are you going to stone me?" (10:32). The point is not only that Jesus is good but also that his works are good. This very goodness causes some to believe in him and others to persecute him and seek his death.

Tuesday in the
Fourth Week of Lent

Ezekiel 47:1-9, 12
Psalm 46:1-8
John 5:1-18

Today's Old Testament lesson from Ezekiel shows us a wonderful vision of streams of living water flowing out of the Temple, down toward the Dead Sea. Like the Great Salt Lake in Utah, the Dead Sea is so saline that nothing can live in it. But the living waters flowing down from the Temple in Ezekiel's vision bring life, making the Dead Sea teem with fish, transforming the surrounding landscape from a barren desert into lush farmland and orchards.

Ezekiel's vision is one of creation itself being renewed and restored by God. For Christians, the streams of living water foreshadow the waters of baptism, by which we become new creations in Christ, receiving our place in the new heaven and new earth that Ezekiel envisions.

Today's Gospel also features healing waters in Jerusalem: the waters of the pool of Bethzatha. The story relates that from time to time, an angel would descend and disturb the waters of the pool. The first person to enter while the waters were churning would be completely healed.

Jesus comes upon an invalid who explains that he can never get into the water quickly enough—someone else always gets there first. Jesus heals the man to demonstrate that whatever healing power the waters may or may not have, he himself is the source of all true healing. Like all of Jesus' healings, this particular miracle points beyond the physical realities of one person's restoration toward the healing of the entire creation, as we see depicted in Ezekiel's vision.

But healing this unnamed sick man comes at a price—Jesus performs it on the Sabbath. When the religious authorities challenge him, Jesus responds that he does on the Sabbath what God himself does on the Sabbath. The authorities seek to kill Jesus because, in their eyes, he has not only violated the Sabbath but has also made himself equal with God.

Today's readings direct our attention to two realities. One is the reality of God's promise of a new creation, in which all our present infirmities and ailments will be healed. But the other reality is the stark reminder that the way to live into this new creation is none other than by following the Way of the Cross.

Ezekiel envisions a restored Temple just as the people of Jerusalem are being forced into exile in Babylon—the smoke from the razing of Jerusalem and the destruction of the Temple still clinging to their clothes and in their nostrils. Ezekiel is given the vision of restoration during a time of defeat and humiliation for God's people. The healing of the invalid at the pool of Bethzatha is also set in the midst of conflict, as it intensifies the opposition to Jesus that ultimately brings about his crucifixion. As we continue through the final weeks of Lent, these readings remind us that we cannot get to Easter Sunday except by way of Good Friday. When we take up the cross and follow Jesus, a whole new creation awaits us.

Wednesday in the
Fourth Week of Lent

Isaiah 49:8-15
Psalm 145:8-19
John 5:19-29

The God revealed in the scriptures of the Old and New Testaments is a God who speaks. By this divine speech, God brings new worlds and realities into being. In Genesis, God fashions the world in six days by speaking all of creation into being. The Christian tradition has always understood this creative Word of God to be the second person of the Holy Trinity, the Son who comes down from heaven in the Incarnation, such that the prologue to John's Gospel declares, "the Word became flesh and lived among us" (1:14a).

In today's Old Testament reading, Isaiah proclaims the power of God's word to liberate and free the children of Israel who are captives in Babylon: "Thus says the LORD: In a time of favor I have answered you, on a day of salvation I have helped you; I have kept you and given you as a covenant to the people, to establish the land, to apportion the desolate heritages; saying to the prisoners,

'Come out,' to those who are in darkness, 'Show yourselves'" (49:8-9a).

Today's reading from John follows on the heels of Jesus' scandalous healing of the invalid at the pool of Bethzatha. When challenged by the religious authorities for healing on the Sabbath, Jesus responds that he does nothing on his own authority but on the authority of his Father in heaven. This authority extends even to raising and judging the dead on the Last Day—"The hour is coming when all who are in their graves will hear his voice and will come out—those who have done good, to the resurrection of life, and those who have done evil, to the resurrection of condemnation" (5:28b-29).

We don't need to wait for the Last Day to hear the voice of the Son of God. Jesus speaks to us even now, calling us from darkness into light, out of bondage into freedom, out of death into life. In the Church's liturgy, Jesus speaks through the reading of the sacred Scriptures and in the voice of the priest at the altar presiding at the holy mysteries. Jesus speaks to us out in the world as well, often through the murmurs and sighs of the most humble and dispossessed of his friends. Not least, Jesus speaks to us in the silence of our hearts when we make room for him in prayer. The challenge for us is simply to listen and respond when we hear his voice.

Thursday in the
Fourth Week of Lent

Exodus 32:7-14
Psalm 106:6-7, 19-23
John 5:30-47

Today's reading from John's Gospel continues the discourse in which Jesus is answering the Jewish religious authorities who have criticized him for healing an invalid on the Sabbath. As we heard in Tuesday's Gospel reading, Jesus justifies his action by saying that he was only doing on the Sabbath what his Father does on the Sabbath—words that harden the authorities' resolve to kill him for making himself equal with God.

In today's reading, Jesus implicitly addresses the question of what witnesses he is able to produce to verify his claim to be the Son of the Father. Refusing to bear witness to himself, Jesus says instead that he has four witnesses who will testify on his behalf.

The first witness is God the Father: "There is another who testifies on my behalf, and I know that his testimony to me is true" (5:32). Jesus continues, "You have never heard his voice or seen his form" (5:37b). So, for those who cannot hear God's voice directly, God's testimony to Jesus must be made manifest through other intermediaries—this is where the remaining three witnesses come in.

The second witness is John the Baptist. At the time of Our Lord's Baptism in the River Jordan, John pointed to Jesus and proclaimed him the Lamb of God: "Here is the Lamb of God who takes away the sin of the world!" (1:29b).

The third witness is the sum total of the signs and wonders Jesus has been performing in his ministry: "The works that the Father has given me to compete, the very works that I am doing, testify on my behalf that the Father has sent me" (5:36b).

The fourth witness consists of the Scriptures, taken as a whole. "You search the Scriptures," Jesus tells his listeners, "because you think that in them you have eternal life; and it is they that testify on my behalf" (5:39). A bit further on, he specifies that Moses himself bears him witness in the Torah: "If you believed Moses, you would believe me, for he wrote about me. But if you do not believe what he wrote, how will you believe what I say" (5:46-47)?

Jesus emphasizes that he needs no human witness. He cites the witness of John the Baptist, the mighty works, and the Scriptures only so that his listeners may have the opportunity to believe in him and be saved.

These same witnesses encourage, enrich, and inform our own faith in Jesus as the Son of God. Just as the first disciples were heartened and stirred by the testimony of John the Baptist, so we have the testimonies of countless faithful women and men who have pointed us to Jesus with their own proclamations of faith. We have as evidence the works Jesus has performed in our lives and the lives of the people around us. And we too have the testimony of the scriptures. While none of these witnesses on its own may be sufficient to confirm our faith in Jesus, all three together are.

Friday in the Fourth Week of Lent

Wisdom 2:1a, 12-24
Psalm 34:15-22
John 7:1-2, 10, 25-30

The daily Eucharistic readings in the latter part of Lent expose us to the mounting tension and opposition to Jesus created by the chief priest and elders. These readings give us glimpses of the controversies that ultimately lead to Jesus' betrayal, arrest, and death.

In our reading from Wisdom, as the ungodly plot against the righteous man, we hear words that uncannily prefigure the words of those who later plot against Jesus. "He professes to have knowledge of God, and calls himself a child of the LORD"(2:13).

The ungodly assume they can discredit the righteous man's pretensions by subjecting him to insults, torture, and death. "Let us condemn him to a shameful death, for, according to what he says, he will be protected" (2:20).

The narrator reflects that the ungodly have strayed blindly from the secret purposes of God. While the ungodly discredit the righteous man and proclaim that God has forsaken him, they fail to understand that the righteous man's death will actually fulfill God's purposes of redemption and salvation.

Contrary to what the ungodly believe, God is with the righteous one who suffers an unjust death. In a way that these blind and ignorant antagonists cannot foresee, God will vindicate the one they seek to put to death.

A similar misunderstanding held by some members of the Jewish community in Jerusalem figures into the reading from John. They question whether Jesus really is the Christ. They know Jesus is from Galilee but have been taught that when the Christ appears, no one will know where he comes from.

The irony here is that even though these naysayers think they know where he comes from—because they know where he lives, who his putative parents are, and the kind of people he consorts with—they really don't know where Jesus ultimately comes from as the only begotten Son of God.

Everything is happening according to God's plan. When the authorities try to arrest Jesus, they fail because his hour has not yet come. In this way, John reminds us that when the authorities finally do succeed in laying hands on Jesus, it will only be because according to God's plan the hour has come—for Jesus' death and resurrection to take place as the means of salvation for the whole world.

The message that calls out to us from today's readings is that even (and maybe especially) in those moments when we think that everything is going wrong, God is still in charge.

We have each suffered disappointments, frustrations, failures, and painful losses—some more than their fair share. Our culture oscillates between two types of response to such misfortunes—on one hand, a therapeutic approach of working through grief by processing and expressing our feelings, and on the other hand, a Stoic approach combining resignation with a grim determination to press on with our lives in the face of all adversity.

Christian faith suggests a third way: seeing the hand of God in the very disappointments and losses. This is not to say that God causes these misfortunes, but that he is present in and through them, working to fulfill his purposes for us as individuals and for all of creation in ways that so often remain hidden from our understanding in this life. The hope that God is indeed present and at work, even in the midst of our most profound suffering, can sustain us. In the moments of sorrow and pain that come upon us, we come close to the sacred heart of Jesus, who bears all our sorrows through his own suffering and death upon the cross.

Saturday in the
Fourth Week of Lent

Jeremiah 11:18-20
Psalm 7:6-11
John 7:37-52

On the last day of the festival, the great day, while Jesus was standing there, he cried out, "Let anyone who is thirsty come to me, and let the one who believes in me drink. As the scripture has said, 'Out of the believer's heart shall flow rivers of living water'" (John 7:37-38).

In this portion of John, we find Jesus in Jerusalem, attending the Feast of Tabernacles. Also known as Sukkot, this Jewish festival lasts for eight days some time in September or October. During this festival, observant Jews build booths or tabernacles, *sukkah*, outdoor makeshift dwellings in which they live. Sukkot is a kind of double festival, as it is a commemoration of the forty years of wandering in the wilderness between the Exodus and the entry into the Promised Land, as well as a celebration of the harvest. The sukkah remind the faithful of their temporary shelters in the Sinai but also provide convenient housing for those working in the fields.

Another feature of the feast during Jesus' time was a daily water ritual. The priests, accompanied by the crowds, would go down to the Pool of Siloam, a reservoir fed by the Gihon Spring, outside the gates of the Temple compound, and return, to blasts of the shofar, bearing vessels of water drawn from this pool. After a procession singing psalms, the priests would pour the water out on the altar. Prayers for rain accompanied this daily libation, which also had the symbolic significance both of remembering the times in the wilderness when God miraculously provided water for his people and of looking forward to the end times, when streams of living water will issue forth from the Temple, irrigating the landscape, causing the barren desert to bloom.

In today's Gospel, Jesus appropriates this water imagery by applying it to himself. He is the source of the living water toward which all these ancient ceremonies point. Those who thirst for the coming of God's Kingdom need only come to him. Jesus goes on to identify this living water with the gift of the Holy Spirit. These words create further division between those in the crowd who accept Jesus as the Prophet or the Messiah and those who are still questioning whether the Messiah can even come from Galilee.

The division extends to the religious authorities themselves. When the chief priests demand to know why Jesus has not been arrested, the Temple police reply,

"Never has anyone spoken like this" (John 7:46). One of the chief priests, Nicodemus, protests that according to the Law, Jesus should not be condemned without a fair hearing. But their minds already made up, the rest of the chief priests reply with derision, "Surely you have not been deceived too, have you?" (7:47).

As Jesus speaks, people divide and line up either for or against him in response to his words. Ironically, however, those who plot against him unwittingly fulfill his prophetic words by setting in motion the sequence of events that will lead to his glorification—his death and resurrection. Today's Gospel challenges us: Will we accept Jesus' invitation to come to him and drink?

Alternative Proper for a Weekday in the Fifth Week in Lent

2 Kings 4:18-21; 32-37
Psalm 17:1-8
John 11:(1-7), 8-44

(NOTE: This proper repeats the Gospel reading for the Fifth Sunday in Lent, Year A, and so is especially suitable for use in Years B and C.)

Death is the basic challenge of human existence. Deep down we resent and rebel against the limitations that our eventual deaths place upon our lives. For example, as we get older, opportunities close as a result of choices that we have made, or indeed, by choices made for us. We have a finite amount of time to try new things. Our time on earth is limited.

We resist the fundamental limitation placed on our lives by death because we have an intuition that we have been created for something else entirely. We have an inexplicable longing for eternal life. Death is the great obstacle to that longing's fulfillment, the final frustration of our deepest hopes and dreams, what Paul calls "the last enemy."

Our resentment of death is compounded by the untimely deaths of young, innocent, vibrant people with work left to finish. Today's readings deal with this phenomenon of premature death. In both cases, however, a miraculous raising of the dead takes place: in the first instance by the ministry of the prophet Elisha and in the second instance by the command of Jesus himself.

The raisings of the Shunammite woman's son and of Lazarus communicate the truth of the Gospel in two ways. First, and most importantly, God's power is stronger than death. Secondly, God's purpose is always to communicate new life.

Reflecting on these stories, the Church has come to see them as anticipatory signs of God's plan to destroy death—to raise up all who have fallen asleep. Both the Shunammite's son and Lazarus were restored to earthly life and eventually died again. But on the last day, God will raise all his children to the eternal life of which Christ's own resurrection is the first fruits.

The irony we see in this story from John is that the raising of Lazarus prompts the Jewish religious authorities to decide to have Jesus put to death. By returning Lazarus to life, Jesus has set in motion a sequence of events leading to his own death and resurrection—which ultimately makes possible our own resurrection from the dead as well.

Monday in the Fifth Week of Lent

Susanna 1-9, 15-29, 34-62 *or* 41-62
Psalm 23
John 8:1-11 *or* 8:12-20

"You shall not bear false witness against your neighbor" (Exodus 20:16). In seeking applications to contemporary life, it is common to interpret this commandment as a prohibition on all forms of lying and untruthfulness, which it is. But it is equally important to remember the commandment's original context in the public administration of justice. In the ancient world (as in the contemporary world), the testimony of false witnesses could lead to those guilty of heinous crimes being found innocent and released or to the innocent being found guilty and wrongly condemned.

Today's Old Testament reading from Susanna tells the story of two false witnesses, elders of the people who have been appointed as judges. Lusting after the happily married Susanna, her harassers threaten to accuse her of adultery with an imaginary paramour if she refuses their advances. Susanna's would-be rapists threaten to accuse her of the same sexual sin they intend to commit.

Susanna refuses their advances, even though she knows that she may die for doing so. The two elders follow through on their threat and accuse her of having sexual relations with a man who is not her husband. Her household erupts with the news of the scandal. A public trial follows, and the gathered assembly condemns Susanna to death. A last-minute intervention comes from the prophet Daniel, who (still a young man in this story) cross-examines the assailants. He reveals the inconsistencies in their sordid lie and saves Susanna from death. The assembly instead executes the corrupt judges for their crime of bearing false witness.

The Gospel for today presents an interesting twist on the problem of false witness. A woman caught in the act of adultery is brought before Jesus. Her accusers ask him whether she should be stoned as the law prescribes. The question is a trap. If Jesus says to stone the adultress, he can be charged with inciting vigilante justice outside the the rule of Roman Law. If Jesus says not to stone her, he can be accused of betraying the Law of Moses.

Jesus sidesteps this trap by declaring, "Let anyone among you who is without sin be the first to throw a stone at her" (John 8:7b). In this way, he effectively redefines the meaning of false witness. Those who have brought the accusation against this woman are themselves guilty of sins just as bad or worse—they are hypocrites with no right to judge anyone. Compassion and mercy trump the letter of the law.

The religious authorities seeking to arrest, try, and condemn Jesus do so even by means of false witnesses. The larger point to bear in mind this week and next week is that Jesus is accused and condemned unjustly. The trial and execution of Jesus violate the Old Testament's deepest standards of justice.

Tuesday in the Fifth Week of Lent

Numbers 21:4-9
Psalm 102:15-22
John 8:21-30

Today's readings provide for an interesting study of biblical typology. (For an explanation of this concept, see the homily for Friday in the Second Week of Lent.)

The reading from Numbers recounts the story of the bronze serpent, an episode occurring toward the end of the Israelites' wandering in the wilderness and taking place in the Wilderness of Sin. The people are (once again) grumbling and complaining that Moses has brought them out of Egypt just to let them die in the desert, hungry, thirsty, and hopeless.

As punishment for this lack of faith, God allows serpents to bite the people, leaving them with burning, poisonous bites. Many die from the bites. Surprisingly, rather than intensifying their grumbling, the children of Israel confess their sins to God and beg Moses to take away the serpents. After nearly forty years in the wilderness, God's chosen people have learned something after all!

God's response to the people's repentance is interesting. Rather than removing the snakes altogether, he commands Moses to fashion a bronze serpent and mount it on a pole placed in full view of any spot in the camp, so that anyone who looks upon it will be healed of their snakebites and live. The underlying theological implication is that while sins may be forgiven, the consequences of sin cannot always be undone.

Why should the visual image of a bronze serpent on a pole be an efficacious means of healing poisonous snakebites? Greek Orthodox theologian Andreas Andreopoulos suggests that in order to be healed, the Israelites must face up to the reality of their sin and its consequences. The bronze serpent symbolizes the snakes sent as punishment for their latest sin as well as the serpent that tempted our first parents in Eden. When the Israelites encounter this visual objectification of their transgression, they are compelled to acknowledge their sin and repent. This is the only way they can find healing, forgiveness, and salvation.

Our Old Testament lesson supplies the background to today's Gospel lesson from John. The deaths of the Israelites in the wilderness from snakebite foreshadow our Lord's words, "I told you that you would die in your sins, for you will die in your sins unless you believe that I am he" (8:24). And Moses lifting up the serpent so that those who look upon it may live foreshadows Jesus' subsequent words: "When you have lifted up the Son of Man, then you will realize that I am he" (8:28a).

The typology we find in this set of stories also depicts our contemporary situation. The serpents in the wilderness represent the temptations that assault us in this life. Without a saving remedy, we will die. But God provides the ultimate remedy—Christ lifted up on the cross. When we look upon the cross, we are led to acknowledge and repent of our sins so that we may receive forgiveness, grace, and healing—just as the snake-bitten Israelites found healing when they looked upon the bronze serpent in the wilderness.

Wednesday in the
Fifth Week of Lent

Daniel 3:14-20, 24-28
Canticle 2 *or* 13
John 8:31-42

As we read through the Old Testament, we notice a certain shift in emphasis as the story progresses. In the early books, the chief problems in the relationship between God and his people are sin and disobedience. From Adam and Eve and Cain and Abel, through Noah and the Flood, to the wanderings in the wilderness, we encounter a God who is gracious and well-disposed toward his people. But those same people are sinful and disobedient to his commands, provoking God to be angry and to dispense judgment.

Further along in the Old Testament narrative, the problem shifts. As a result of the Babylonian conquest of Jerusalem in 586 BCE, the Jewish people become subjects of a series of foreign overlords—Babylonian, Persian, Hellenistic Greek, and Roman. More and more, the chief religious problem is less the people's disobedience to God—though that remains a serious problem to be sure—as the cost of obedience when foreign masters require the children of Israel to disregard their covenant with God, to disobey God's laws, and to worship other gods.

In today's reading from Daniel, King Nebuchadnezzar has cast three young men—Shadrach, Meshach, and Abednego—into a lit furnace because of their refusal to worship a false god. Their refusal of Nebuchadnezzar's demand illustrates two seemingly conflicting convictions. On the one hand, these three young men believe deeply in the power of God to deliver them. On the other hand— and this point should not be overlooked—Shadrach, Meshach, and Abednego are prepared to die an agonizing death rather than forsake the God of Israel. For these two reasons, their story continues to inspire generations of faithful Jewish and Christian martyrs who are willing to die rather than renounce their faith.

Shadrach, Meshach, and Abednego are a trinity of types for Jesus Christ, who was likewise faithful unto death in steadfast obedience to God's mission for him to redeem the world. Some traditions of Christian interpretation have seen in the mysterious fourth figure who appears in the flames a manifestation of Jesus, the Son of God. The miraculous deliverance of Shadrach, Meshach, and Abednego anticipates the ultimate miraculous deliverance of Christ from death and the grave.

This wonderful Old Testament story of the three young men in the fiery furnace offers us the reassurance that although we may suffer terribly for our adherence to the faith in this life, Jesus will always walk with us through the fire. In Christ Jesus, we have the promise of deliverance and vindication.

Thursday in the Fifth Week of Lent

Genesis 17:1-8
Psalm 105:4-11
John 8:51-59

Today, we see Jesus in the precincts of the Temple, in a dispute with Jewish religious authorities during the Feast of Tabernacles (*Sukkot*). The tension is rising to the boiling point as Jesus' opponents press him to clarify who he claims to be. Jesus declares that those who keep his word will never see death. Jesus is talking here about spiritual death, but his opponents misunderstand his words as referring to literal physical death. They challenge him: "Are you greater than our father Abraham, who died? The prophets also died. Who do you claim to be?" (John 8:53).

Jesus responds with a mysterious statement: "Your ancestor Abraham rejoiced that he would see my day; he saw it and was glad" (8:56). His opponents are incredulous: "You are not yet fifty years old, and have you seen Abraham?" (8:57). In response, Jesus makes a startling and dramatic proclamation of his own pre-existence: "Very truly, I tell you, before Abraham was, I am" (8:58). Here Jesus invokes the Old Testament name of God (I AM), identifying himself with God.

This proclamation helps explain the lectionary compilers' choice of the Old Testament reading. The Church has traditionally understood "the Lord" who speaks with Abraham in the Book of Genesis as none other than the Word or *Logos* of God, the Second Person of the Holy Trinity, who ultimately takes flesh and becomes incarnate as Jesus of Nazareth. By this reading, Jesus not only existed before Abraham but also actually appeared to Abraham. In this way, again, Jesus can say that Abraham rejoiced to see his day.

Jesus' claim to divinity is unmistakable. It is no wonder that the Jewish religious authorities, not accepting this claim, accuse him of blasphemy and want him dead. He escapes their clutches this time because it is not yet his hour. But the pattern that ultimately leads to Jesus' death has been set all the more firmly.

Friday in the Fifth Week of Lent

Jeremiah 20:7-13
Psalm 18:1-7
John 10:31-42

In today's Old Testament reading, we learn that the prophet Jeremiah has been subjected to severe persecution and suffering. He complains to God: "O LORD, you have enticed me, and I was enticed; you have overpowered me, and you have prevailed (20:7a). His complaint is understandable—Jeremiah has done his best to obey God—to speak the words God has given him to speak. In return for his obedience, the poor man has become a laughingstock, an object of derision. It would have been much easier for Jeremiah to have kept his mouth shut so he could enjoy a quiet life in the company of congenial friends.

Herein lies the rub: Try as Jeremiah might to be safe and navigate a prudent course, he cannot. In spite of himself, he is driven to speak the word of the Lord even though the consequences of doing so are the last things Jeremiah wants to suffer.

In the end, all Jeremiah can do is commit his cause to God, trusting that he will finally be vindicated: "But the LORD is with me like a dread warrior; therefore my persecutors will stumble, and they will not prevail" (20:11a). And so, having begun by complaining and accusing God, he concludes with a song of praise: "Sing to the LORD; praise the LORD! For he has delivered the life of the needy from the hands of the evildoers" (20:13).

Like Jeremiah, Jesus knows what it costs to speak the truth—and to do God's work. In today's Gospel, Jesus confronts those who want to stone him to death: "I have shown you many good works from the Father. For which of these are you going to stone me?" (10:32). Even though he escapes those who are trying to kill him, this incident foreshadows the approaching moment when he will indeed be betrayed, arrested, tried, condemned, and crucified, and all for speaking the truth and doing the works of his Father in heaven.

As we approach Holy Week, these readings remind us of the cost of fidelity and obedience to God. That cost can be steep indeed. Yet, no matter what we may have to suffer for doing what we believe to be God's will for us, the words of Jeremiah echo a reassurance of ultimate vindication and victory: "Sing to the Lord; praise the Lord! For he has delivered the life of the needy from the hands of the evildoers."

Saturday in the Fifth Week of Lent

Ezekiel 37:21-28
Psalm 85:1-7
John 11:45-53

The readings for today bring us to the climactic moment in John's Gospel when the Jewish authorities decide that Jesus must die. In Matthew, Mark, and Luke, the precipitating event for Jesus' condemnation is the expulsion of the moneychangers and vendors from the Temple. But in John's Gospel, the straw that breaks the camel's back is the raising of Lazarus.

In a story dripping with irony, we find Jesus manifesting the most dramatic and compelling sign yet that he is the Son of God. Instead of believing in him, the authorities decide Jesus must be done away with.

The chief priests and elders have become so practiced at maneuvering between the imperial power of Rome and their own local autonomy, that most of them are unable to recognize that the Messiah has entered into their midst. Their only thought is that popular, miracle-working, messianic figures wreak havoc when they are left unchecked: "What are we to do? This man is performing many signs. If we let him go on like this, everyone will believe in him, and the Romans will come and destroy both our holy place and our nation" (11:47b-48). Caiaphas, a politician if there ever was one, cryptically remarks: "You know nothing at all! You do not understand that it is better for you to have one man die for the people than to have the whole nation destroyed" (11:49b-50).

There was a belief in first-century Israel (dating back at least to the Maccabean era) that the martyrdom of a righteous man could atone for the sins of the people and thereby avert God's wrath. But it seems unlikely that Caiaphas is thinking any such high-minded religious thoughts. His words almost certainly reflect instrumental calculations of political expediency: better to be rid of one troublemaker through questionable means than to court political and military catastrophe.

Unbeknownst to Caiaphas, however, he is being used in his capacity as high priest to speak a truth that he neither understands nor intends. Although he doesn't know what he is saying, Caiaphas unwittingly prophesies that Jesus will die for the children of Israel and for all God's children scattered abroad.

God is working his purpose out, even through the self-serving machinations of Judean power politics. Contrary to the expectations of those plotting against Jesus, his death will not represent the removal of a nuisance to the powers-that-be but the beginning of God's cosmic victory. And all this is happening according to a plan that neither Caiaphas nor those around him understand. It is into the mystery of that victory that the liturgies of Holy Week bid us enter in the days ahead.

Monday in Holy Week

Isaiah 42:1-9
Psalm 36:5-11
Hebrews 9:11-15
John 12:1-11

Bethany, identified with the modern town of El-Eizariya on the Mount of Olives, is about a mile and a half from Jerusalem. John identifies Bethany as the home of Mary, Martha, and Lazarus, whom Jesus raised from the dead. In modern-day El-Eizariya, you can still see Lazarus's reputed tomb. On Palm Sunday, Jesus and the disciples approach Jerusalem from the villages of Bethany and Bethphage. According to Matthew and Mark, Bethany is the place where Jesus and the disciples lodged during their final week in Jerusalem.

It makes sense that John would identify Mary of Bethany as the woman who anoints Jesus with costly ointment of pure nard. All four gospels record some version of this incident, although they differ on the details. In John's telling of this story, Jesus' anointing by Mary of Bethany takes place amidst the rising tension that will soon lead to Jesus' betrayal, arrest, and death.

While Jesus and his friends are gathered and eating supper, Mary enters the room to make her offering of love and comfort to Jesus. When she anoints Jesus, Judas complains that the ointment should have been sold and the proceeds given to the poor. Judas's derision of this act points in an anticipatory way to the role he will soon play—betraying Jesus to the authorities.

Jesus' rebuke of Judas points explicitly to his approaching death: "Leave her alone. She bought it so that she might keep it for the day of my burial. You always have the poor with you, but you do not always have me" (John 12:7). This saying is sometimes misused to suggest that Jesus condemns generosity to the poor, whereas it has precisely the opposite implication: After he is gone, his Church will have until the end of time to take care of the poor, a never-ending obligation.

This story makes clear Jesus' raising up Lazarus from the dead has made them both celebrities. The religious authorities have already determined that Jesus must be put to death. As Lazarus' testimony is leading many to follow Jesus, the powers that be also decide to put Lazarus to death—although there is no subsequent indication in scripture or tradition that they were successful in doing so.

In the midst of all this conflict, the central action is the loving deed of Mary of Bethany anointing the feet of Jesus and wiping them with her hair, so that the whole house is filled with the fragrance of the ointment. The Greek title "Christ" and the Hebrew title "Messiah" both mean "Anointed One." Although Jesus interprets Mary's action in terms of his coming burial, it also visually symbolizes who he is: the Anointed One of God.

Tuesday in Holy Week

Isaiah 49:1-7
Psalm 71:1-14
I Corinthians 1:18-31
John 12:20-36

Jesus answered, "This voice has come for your sake, not for mine. Now is the judgment of this world; now the ruler of this world will be driven out. And I, when I am lifted up from the earth, will draw all people to myself." He said this to indicate the kind of death he was to die (John 12:30-33).

As we approach the Sacred Triduum (Maundy Thursday, Good Friday, and Holy Saturday), the Eucharistic readings for Holy Week draw our attention to aspects of Jesus' impending suffering and death. John especially stresses an element of paradox that can be seen in two ways in today's Gospel.

The first way we see this paradox revealed concerns judgment. Those conspiring to put Jesus to death see themselves as the ones dispensing and executing judgment. All those involved in the proceedings (Caiaphas, the Jewish religious authorities, Pontius Pilate and his Roman officials and soldiers, Herod) know that they are responsible for maintaining order in their remote corner of the Roman Empire. To keep the peace, they must exercise judicial authority and condemn with extreme prejudice anyone who poses a threat to the status quo. In the Old Testament, this process is referred to as "casting out"—those found guilty of transgressions are removed from the community, killed or driven into exile.

Speaking of his impending passion and death, Our Lord turns this language completely upside down. "Now is the judgment of this world; now the ruler of this world will be driven out. And I, when I am lifted up from the earth, will draw all people to myself" (12:31-32). The paradox is that in the very act of pronouncing judgment on Jesus, the powers of this world bring themselves under judgment. In the very act of condemning Jesus, they bring themselves under condemnation. It is as though their exercise of judgment boomerangs back on itself with infinite magnitude. And it is the ruler of this world, the devil, who is ultimately cast out as the result of his futile attempt to cast out the Son of God.

The second part of the paradox has to do with the crucifixion. "Jesus answered them, 'The hour has come for the Son of Man to be glorified'" (12:23). In the ancient world, there was no death more shameful and humiliating than crucifixion. Yet in John's Gospel, our Lord speaks of it as his *glorification*. The phrase "be lifted up" would normally have been understood to refer to triumph or exaltation, but instead our Lord uses it to refer to being hung on the cross. In this way, Jesus predicts that his crucifixion will have the absolute opposite effect of what his executioners intend. They aim to degrade him; instead, Jesus is glorified. They aim to make him an outcast that people will go out of their way to avoid; in the ancient world, people did their best not to go near crucifixions. However, what is made manifest on Easter Day has been true all along. Even from the cross, Jesus reigns as king. The cross is the judgment by which the ruler of this world is cast out. And lifted up on the cross, Jesus draws us all to himself.

Wednesday in Holy Week

Isaiah 50:4-9a
Psalm 70
Hebrews 12:1-3
John 13:21-32

One theme running throughout today's readings is that Jesus undergoes his sufferings freely and willingly. As one of the Eucharistic prayers of the contemporary Roman Rite puts it, at the time he was betrayed "he entered willingly into his Passion."

In our reading from Isaiah, the prophet emphasizes that the Servant of the Lord does not attempt to run away from the sufferings he must undergo: "I gave my back to those who struck me, and my cheeks to those who pulled out the beard; I did not hide my face from insult and spitting" (50:6).

The reading from the letter to the Hebrews describes Jesus as the model of endurance: "…let us run with perseverance the race that is set before us, looking to Jesus the pioneer and perfecter of our faith, who for the sake of the joy that was set before him endured the cross, disregarding its shame, and has taken his seat at the right hand of the throne of God" (12:1b-2).

In the Gospel lesson, the scene from John's account of the Last Supper shows us that Jesus knows full well that Judas is about to betray him and nonetheless permits events to escalate and run their course. When Judas goes out into the night, Jesus sees approaching glory: "Now the Son of Man has been glorified, and God has been glorified in him. If God has been glorified in him, God will also glorify him in himself and will glorify him at once" (13:31-32).

Taken together, today's readings remind us that as horrific and gruesome as the Passion of our Lord clearly is, it is not something that he is forced to undergo against his will. Jesus does not have some crazy death wish, but when death comes for him, he accepts it as God's plan for the redemption of the world. He freely yields himself to those who will betray, arrest, try, condemn, torture, and execute him. He could run away, resist, fight, call down legions of angels to save him. But he does not do any of these things.

Jesus is a victim, but he is not a helpless victim. He willingly accepts and offers up his sufferings on behalf of the whole of humanity to fulfill his God-given mission. For this redemption—this inexpressibly unique and completely unmerited gift—we owe him our never-ending thanks and praise.

And perhaps Jesus' example of suffering may strengthen us to freely accept whatever comes our way as we fulfill our duties to God and our neighbor in this life—even if such sufferings for us take the form of nothing more than mild inconveniences. When we consider what Jesus has done for us, and at such great cost, then can any cost be too great for whatever he might ask of us in return?

Maundy Thursday

Exodus 12:1-4, (5-10), 11-14
Psalm 116:1, 10-17
1 Corinthians 11:23-26
John 13:1-17, 31b-35

The night Jesus is betrayed begins with supper. During this meal, our Lord says and does some unexpected things, which no doubt puzzle those present. Before supper, Jesus washes his disciples' feet—an action more appropriate to a servant than a host. During (and after) supper, at the appropriate times for the blessings, Jesus speaks mysterious words about the bread being his body and the wine being his blood.

In the fullness of time, the disciples will come to understand what Jesus is telling them. The broken bread indeed becomes his body; the wine becomes his blood. Jesus knows that his crucifixion will be the fulfillment of his mission on earth, and so he institutes this rite to bring that moment back to his followers in every century henceforth until the end of time.

Following the way of the cross in Jesus' footsteps is an entire way of life entailing fellowship with other

Christians—a fellowship intimately manifested in the corporate act of eating and drinking together—by breaking bread and drinking from a common cup. In and through their table fellowship, Christians recognize their unity with one another and with the risen Lord present in their midst.

By receiving the bread and wine that have become the Body and Blood of the Lord, the Church itself is transformed and reconstituted as the Body of Christ on earth. Saint Teresa of Avila, the great mystic, maintains that, "Christ has no body now on earth but yours, no hands but yours, no feet but yours." We are called as Christians, as members of Jesus' body—this miraculous extension of the Incarnation—to do in our day what he did in his: Proclaim good news to the poor, heal the sick, and comfort the afflicted.

This is where the foot washing comes into play. As Jesus explains to his disciples, if he (as their Lord and Master) assumes the role of a servant and washes their feet, so they must also do for one another. The Church is called to be a community characterized not only by eating and drinking together but also by mutual self-sacrifice and loving service. By washing his disciples' feet, Jesus exemplifies for us what it means to be his Body in the world. Jesus comes among us as one who serves, and we are likewise called to be servants—of God, of one another, and of our neighbors.

At supper with his disciples the night before he suffers, Our Lord gives us a gift and an example. The gift he gives us is the sacrament of his Body and Blood, by which he nourishes and sustains us with his very life. The example he asks us to follow is that of humble service, enacted in the simple task of foot washing, through which he teaches us how to be his Body in the world.

Good Friday

Isaiah 52:13—53:12
Psalm 22
Hebrews 10:16-25 *or* Hebrews 4:14-16, 5:7-9
John 18:1—19:42

During Jesus' trial as related in John's Gospel, Pontius Pilate declares three times, "I find no case against him." Another translation of "case against him" might be "crime in him" (RSV), or "basis for a charge against him" (NIV).

According to the understanding of Jewish law that prevailed during Jesus' lifetime, to declare something three times was to make that statement irrevocable and binding. The irony here is that Pilate declares Jesus innocent three times—and hands him over for crucifixion anyway. Pilate perverts justice by openly condemning an innocent man to death.

The problem of unjust and undeserved suffering remains a problem across the wide expanse of human history. For example, when we witness in war the wholesale slaughter and maiming of civilians, or the refusal to acknowledge the humanity of refugees fleeing to safe haven, our inmost selves cry out to heaven in protest: "Why, Lord, why?"

Down through the centuries, second-rate philosophers and religious teachers have proposed facile solutions to this problem. Suffering, they say, is good for us. It strengthens our character and makes us better people. But this idea is one of the most pernicious lies we have taught ourselves to believe. During the Second World War, British pacifist Vera Brittain wrote that, far from strengthening character and ennobling people, most unjust suffering has precisely the opposite effect. Unjust and unjustified suffering brutalizes and dehumanizes its victims, creating a legacy of bitterness, resentment, hatred, and thirst for revenge.

The one exception, Brittain maintains, is when such suffering is freely accepted by victims who offer it up sacrificially in the service of a higher cause. In that case alone, unjust suffering has the potential to become redemptive and transformative. But very few people have the capacity for such sacrificial self-offering.

The Gospel we proclaim on Good Friday is that Jesus Christ, the Incarnate Son of God, fully human and fully divine, is the one and only innocent victim who has ever accepted unjust suffering and death with such perfect humility and resignation that his offering of himself on the cross constitutes, to quote *The Book of Common Prayer, 1979*, "A full, perfect, and sufficient sacrifice, oblation, and satisfaction, for the sins of the whole world" (p. 334).

The Church has never defined as dogma any of the many competing theories of precisely how Jesus' death on the cross accomplishes the forgiveness of sins and the reconciliation of a fallen world to God. To the extent that we find these theories helpful, we are free to make use of them. If we find them unhelpful, we are free to discard them and move on. Ultimately, our redemption by the cross is a mystery that defies all attempts at exhaustive explanation. Still, despite the unpopularity of "atonement theology" in certain theological circles today, the cross remains central to the Christian doctrine of salvation.

Two consequences follow for us in living out our calling as Christians. The first is realizing that following Jesus means walking in the way of the cross. When we find ourselves facing some injury, disease, or other calamity that entails pain and loss, we can accept it as a way of being close to Jesus. This acceptance comes to us by divine grace—a gift of the Holy Spirit. By staying close to Jesus, we can bear anything for his sake.

Secondly, however, while we may freely accept the path of redemptive suffering for ourselves, we have no right to impose it on others. There is something particularly cruel and wicked about telling those in pain that acceptance of their suffering makes them better people. It is downright blasphemous to inflict pain and suffering on the pretext that suffering is somehow good for the victims.

On the contrary, through the centuries, the Church's best wisdom has concluded that our Christian obligation is to do everything we can to prevent, stop, and relieve the unjust suffering of innocent victims whenever and wherever we encounter it in the world. Our mission is one of healing, reconciliation, restoration, and justice.

At this time in our history, Christians have a particular obligation to work to end the systemic injustice that disproportionately victimizes the poor as well as racial and ethnic minorities. Yet we have the assurance that whenever innocent victims suffer unjustly, Jesus suffers with them. And when we minister to innocent victims with compassion and love, we minister to Christ himself.

The Great Vigil of Easter

Genesis 1:1—2:2
Psalm 33:1-11 *or* Psalm 36:5-10
Genesis 7:1-5, 11-18; 8:6-18; 9:8-13
Psalm 46
Genesis 22:1-18
Psalm 33:12-22 *or* Psalm 16
Exodus 14:10—15:1
Canticle 8
Isaiah 4:2-6
Psalm 122
Isaiah 55:1-11
Canticle 9
Ezekiel 36:24-28
Psalm 42:1-7 *or* Canticle 9
Ezekiel 37:1-14
Psalm 30 *or* Psalm 143
Zephaniah 3:12-20
Psalm 98 *or* Psalm 126

Romans 6:3-11
Psalm 114
Matthew 28:1-10

On Easter morning we celebrate the finding of the empty
tomb and the resurrection appearances. However, during

the Great Vigil we focus on the deep mystery of what happens in the dark solitude of the tomb before dawn: the Resurrection itself. On this most holy night, then, it seems appropriate to say a few words about Christ's descent into hell, also known as the harrowing of hell.

The Apostles' Creed states that after Jesus died and was buried, "he descended into hell, and on the third day he rose again." Several New Testament passages mention this descent into hell, albeit briefly.

In his sermon on the day of Pentecost in the Acts of the Apostles, Peter quotes Psalm 16, "You will not abandon me to the grave, nor let your holy one see the Pit" (16:10). Peter then explains, "Forseeing this, David spoke of the resurrection of the Messiah, saying, 'He was not abandoned to Hades, nor did his flesh experience corruption'" (Acts 2:31). These words suggest that Christ's soul went to Hades but was not abandoned there, while his body remained incorrupt in the tomb. In Peter's first Epistle, we are told that Jesus was "put to death in the flesh, but made alive in the spirit; in which also he went and made a proclamation to the spirits in prison" (3:18-19). A bit later, he adds: "For this is the reason the gospel was proclaimed even to the dead, so that, though they had been judged in the flesh as everyone else is judged, they might live in the spirit as God does" (4:6). Paul writes to the Christians in Ephesus, that Christ "descended into the lower parts of the earth," and then later "ascended far above all the heavens, that he might fill all things" (Ephesians 4:9-10).

One last allusion to the harrowing of hell occurs when the New Testament speaks of Christ being raised from the dead; the phrase "from the dead" in the literal meaning of the Greek text is not "from the state of death," but rather "from among the dead ones." Based on these texts, the Church's traditional understanding is that when Jesus died and was placed in the tomb, his soul left his body and descended into *Sheol* (Hebrew), or *Hades* (Greek). Neither term refers to a place of eternal damnation and punishment but rather a shadowy realm where the spirits of the dead are imprisoned, awaiting redemption.

Rather than becoming imprisoned, Jesus tramples down the very gates of hell, crushing the power of the devil, preaching the Good News, and freeing the souls of the dead. Finally, his own soul ascends and rejoins his body in the tomb, raising it to the new and eternal life of the Resurrection. This sublime imagery points to at least three truths crucial to Christian faith.

First, Jesus truly experiences death. From his conception and birth, he goes through all the stages of human existence, to the grave and beyond. In this way, Jesus is present for us in every stage of our life and death. Even as we go down into the grave, he is there waiting for us. Not even death can separate us from the love of God in Christ Jesus.

Second, by descending into hell, Christ has made his presence known in every part of creation, from the highest heaven to the lowest depths of the earth. In particular, by preaching the Gospel to those who had died before him, Jesus shows that his offer of eternal salvation extends to all people in all times and places.

Third, by ascending from hell after descending there, Jesus conquers death and the grave: a victory that will be made manifest when he appears on Easter Day; a victory in which we share by being baptized into Christ's Body, the Church.

Tomorrow morning we will celebrate the discovery of the empty tomb and the appearances of the Risen Lord to his followers. But this evening, we celebrate the Mystery of Christ's Resurrection itself in the words of the *Exsultet*: "This is the night, when Christ broke the bonds of death and hell, and rose victorious from the grave" (*The Book of Common Prayer, 1979*, p. 287).

About the Author

John D. Alexander has been Rector of St. Stephen's Episcopal Church in Providence, Rhode Island, since 2000. He previously served parishes in Wayne, Pennsylvania, and Staten Island, New York. He received his doctorate in Christian ethics from Boston University in 2014 and also holds advanced degrees from the Johns Hopkins University, Virginia Theological Seminary, and Nashotah Theological Seminary. He currently serves as superior of the American Region of the Society of Mary, an international devotional society in the Anglo-Catholic tradition. This is his second book for Forward Movement and can be a companion to his first, *Dawn from on High: Homilies for the Weekdays of Advent, Christmas, and Epiphany.*

About Forward Movement

Forward Movement is committed to inspiring disciples and empowering evangelists. While we produce great resources like this book, Forward Movement is not a publishing company. We are a ministry.

Our mission is to support you in your spiritual journey, to help you grow as a follower of Jesus Christ. Publishing books, daily reflections, studies for small groups, and online resources is an important way that we live out this ministry. More than a half million people read our daily devotions through *Forward Day by Day*, which is also available in Spanish (*Adelante Día a Día*) and Braille, online, as a podcast, and as an app for your smartphones or tablets. It is mailed to more than fifty countries, and we donate nearly 30,000 copies each quarter to prisons, hospitals, and nursing homes. We actively seek partners across the Church and look for ways to provide resources that inspire and challenge.

A ministry of The Episcopal Church for eighty years, Forward Movement is a nonprofit organization funded by sales of resources and gifts from generous donors. To learn more about Forward Movement and our resources, please visit us at www.forwardmovement.org (or www.venadelante.org).

We are delighted to be doing this work and invite your prayers and support.